A native of Somerset, author and journalist **David Stuckey** worked on newspapers in Hampshire and Worcester before moving to Liverpool in 1972. Currently on the features staff of the *Liverpool Daily Post*, he has known the Spinners a long while and been a folk music fan even longer. Married with two children, he now lives in Lancashire, and this is his first book under his own name.

Dedicated to my mother and the memory of my father

My thanks go to five very special entertainers, their families, friends and fans who have made this profile possible. May everyone find as much enjoyment in reading it, as I had in researching and writing it.

D.L.S.

The SPINNERS

Fried Bread and Brandy-O!

David Stuckey

Robson Books

Acknowledgements

Grateful thanks to the *Liverpool Daily Post and Echo*, Yorkshire Television, Border Television, the BBC, the *Lincolnshire Echo*, Williamson Photographers of Warley, and Guyse Williams of Heswall, for help with the photographs.

FIRST PUBLISHED IN GREAT BRITAIN IN HARDBACK IN 1983 BY ROBSON BOOKS LTD., BOLSOVER HOUSE, 5-6 CLIPSTONE STREET, LONDON W1P 7EB. THIS ROBSON PAPERBACK EDITION FIRST PUBLISHED IN 1985.

British Library Cataloguing in Publication Data

Stuckey, David
The Spinners.
1. Spinners, The
I. Title
784.5'0092'2 ML421.S/

ISBN 0 86051 334 3

Printed in Hungary

Contents

Foreword

Over twenty years ago I and my family spent an evening at the Spinners club in Liverpool, and never forgot it. The strong forthright quality of sound, the wide variety of folks and songs — like British beer, traditional at its best. I haven't heard them much since, but am glad to see by this book that they have been able to survive, grow, travel, while still staying close to their roots. May their friends in many places get to know them better through these pages, and may the Liverpool beer keep flowing.

But no paper and print could ever capture that quality of sound . . .

Feb. '83
Beacon
NY
USA

Pete Seeger 平和

Introduction

'This Is Your Life . . .' When Eamonn Andrews surprised me with those words some years ago, it was the signal for an evening of very pleasant surprises — the final one being an appearance by the Spinners, who easily persuaded me to join them on washboard for a quick chorus of 'Coney Island Washboard Roundalay'.

Most guests make an effort to be on 'This Is Your Life', to pay tribute to the willing victim, and mine were no exception. The Spinners even postponed a concert date that evening just to be there, and I was very flattered and grateful.

Washboard playing has long been a hobby of mine, reflecting a life-long love of jazz, and the Spinners, as well as being supreme folk singers, also share that love.

I have known them for most of the years they have been together as a group, and we have shared lots of fun as I've been invited to strum my washboard with them on several television shows from the Octagon, Bolton, and on several radio shows too. I have also appeared with them at the Royal Festival Hall, and they asked me to repeat 'Coney Island' on their *Spinners in Town* LP.

Tony, Hughie, Mick and Cliff have always been very kind to me and they have become valued friends in that time. I am extremely fond of them — after all, they are fellow countrymen of mine, for Liverpool is my home too — and I greatly admire all they have achieved.

So this is their life, a testament to hard work and success. No one deserves success more, for their secret is rooted in a sincere and consistent approach to entertainment, which never fails to win over family audiences everywhere. And long may they continue to do so.

'Fried Bread and Brandy-O'

'Fried bread and brandy-o . . .' The spotlight picks out Mick, short, nippy, the silver fox of the foursome as he dashes centre-stage. He launches into the familiar Spinners version of an old Liverpool playground rhyme which has been their introduction tune for many years, and the others follow on stage on cue . . . Hugh, bubbling, bouncy, energetic; Cliff, more languid, relaxed, serene; and Tony, their tower of strength, the whistling Pied Piper.

With John McCormick slipping in behind them on bass, they launch into their first sing-along number, testing the strength of the audience, its mood, its willingness to engage itself as well as be entertained.

The Spinners have lost count over the years of the number of times they've been told, 'You'll never get this lot to sing.' And they've yet to find an audience of which that is true. By the end of any Spinners evening the majority of the audience is aware that they've not just been to a concert, but to a gigantic group session in happiness therapy.

That has been the Spinners' essential appeal and contribution over the years — spreading happiness and a love of folk music that is as infectious as it is sincere. It is a recipe which has kept them at the top for twenty-five years, as the biggest and best-loved names in folk entertainment.

Whether any of them actually planned it that way, or believed it could really last this long, is another matter . . .

'So he comes to me and says: "I'm going to form a folk group and I'd like you to be in it." I thought, man, this guy is mad!'

Cliff Hall well remembers the day Tony Davis dropped that particular bombshell. It was one thing for this good-looking, good-humoured expatriate Jamaican to strum his old black guitar and sing the country music hits he had come to love in the privacy of his own home. It was quite another to get up in front of a folk-club audience and do it in public.

He was joining two teachers who had gravitated together through a mutual love of jazz and skiffle, a ship's engineer turned guitar-maker, plus Tony's sister Joan and his wife Beryl. They were later joined by a fancy-goods clerk launched into the folk orbit by a chance meeting on a Liverpool bus with Dan Dare, and a student teacher from the Bronte country, who played a nifty mandolin.

When Cliff went home to Jamaica and told his folks he was going to be a professional entertainer, they hooted with laughter. When his wife begged for a little peace, driven to distraction by his practising, he would say, more in hope than conviction: 'Be quiet. I'm going to make my living out of this one day.'

Hardly, on the face of it, a recipe for success, let alone lasting success. And yet, this same heady mix of improbables distilled into the captivating and enduring success that was and is the Spinners.

It began in their Liverpool home at — of all things — a Conservative fête, and their sound is still very much part of the Mersey music scene, though it has also captivated audiences in concert halls, major and minor, in Britain and abroad.

If Cliff's conversion to performing needed prompting, Tony Davis's was natural. Inspired with a love of singing by his family background, and turned on to jazz while still at school, he got together a number of jazz combos while in his teens and at college, playing cheerful clarinet.

Mick Groves' musical path was more formal, via church choir and the Scouts, before he met up with Tony at teacher training college, and learned guitar. Both would probably still be jazz musicians today if it hadn't been for Lonnie Donegan. And they would still be doing the rounds of folk clubs if it hadn't been for Flanders and Swann.

As for Hughie Jones — a shy lad who brought his guitar along to the Spinners' folk basement because that was the way to get in free — he was persuaded to perform, and found a latent talent not only to sing immaculate unaccompanied ballads but also to write ballads of delicacy and style.

Weave all these threads together and you have the enduring tapestry of appealing enjoyment and entertainment that is the Spinners.

In my Liverpool home

Monday night in Paradise . . . posh accents and posher cars jostle outside Liverpool's Holiday Inn, while on the other side of the street, next door to the smoothly efficient buzz of Radio Merseyside, in the upper lounge of the Triton pub, the Spinners are entertaining the faithful.

Ever since their days as a fledgling folk group, the boys have had a Liverpool base, a club of their own. It is as much their home as the houses they live in, attended by their loyalest fans and their sternest critics. The Triton is the third city venue for the Spinners' folk club. Once upon a time they would try to come back to the club each week to perform, to listen, to relax. Now they make it once a month, but the club still functions weekly as a nursery for fresh talent and a meeting-place for old favourites.

If the Spinners want to try a new number or a different routine, they usually do it at the club, knowing the reaction they'll get will be honest, frank, and tinged with that brand of humour which is the Liverpudlian trademark.

Scouse humour is rightly renowned — it presents a view of life that is both revealing and sardonic in a gentle, mocking way. Many believe the Beatles first put Liverpool on the entertainment map, but long before Merseybeat and the hysterical 1960s, there was Tommy Handley, Arthur Askey, Deryck Guyler, and many more, teaching the country how to laugh at adversity. It is no accident that two of today's most sought-after comedy writers, Eddie Braben and Carla Lane, are Liverpool bred — as are a number of top comics, including Ken Dodd, Jimmy Tarbuck and Tom O'Connor.

They provide a slice of life refreshingly honest in its appeal and in its humour, reflected in the average Liverpudlian. Over the years the Spinners have benefited from that honesty, and learnt from that frank family atmosphere.

'Saw you on the box last Tuesday,' one lady says to Tony. 'You were last!' (Scouse for 'rubbish'.) Mick blurts out: 'I'd like to dedicate this next number to the best football team in the land — Manchester United,' and is greeted with howls of derision for a soccer evangelist with a lost cause.

There's much good-humoured banter between them, too — from Cliff's quiet quips to Hughie's dry wit . . . 'That's good, that — playing in one key and singing in another. How do you do it?'

John McCormick doesn't escape either. After an ambitious riff, Mick says: 'Wow — he's not just a pretty bass then.' And they launch into 'Muleskinner Blues': 'Good morning, captain . . .' eliciting the inevitable camp reply, 'Hello, sailor!'

Mick all but loses his way introducing one number and Hughie says: 'That was a contrived link.' 'I know — I was wrestling with it all through the last song.' 'That accounts for your playing then!'

Cliff, in his soft Caribbean voice, is explaining the lyrics of a West Indian song, and finds himself competing with the noise of a passing juggernaut heading for the docks. Hughie yells through the open window, 'Shut up! Cliff's talking!'

They've become the butt of many good-humoured jests over the years too. A stock Liverpool clubland comic's joke at one time was: 'I've met the man who cured the Spinners of "Whip Jamboree".'

While Liverpool has remained their home, it has not always been kind to them. The Jacaranda Club in the city centre was a favourite haunt of folkies, artists and performers in the early 1960s and, stopping off there late one night after a gig, the boys parked their van opposite so they could keep an eye on it — but still lost four guitars and a case of Cliff's harmonicas that night. Over the years, they have lost other instruments: Tony's valuable banjo, one of only sixty made by W. Lund in Nelson and Colne seventy-five years earlier, also went missing for a fortnight in 1978, shortly before the Spinners left for Norway in the Tall Ships Race, to play before King Olav. It was lost after a club night at the Triton, but turned up after a newspaper appeal.

On another occasion, Hughie also had his guitar stolen — but the thief seemingly only wanted the case (he took Mick's as well) and left the £300 guitar in a field, where it was found next morning. Fortunately the night was a dry one; rain would certainly have ruined it.

I met the West Country group the Wurzels at a Sunday seaside show in Great Yarmouth, and conversation got round to the Spinners. 'There's no denying they're terrific artists, with massive appeal,' said Pete Budd, the trio's Adge Cutler soundalike and banjo player. 'Mind you, I must admit some of what they does bores me to tears.'

'Oh, I wouldn't say that,' added Tony Baylis, their tall laconic bass player. 'Everything they does bores me to tears!'

Ah well, you can't win 'em all . . . but then, the Spinners have been together a long time and built up a relationship among themselves and with their fans that has weathered the years. It is a relationship which enables them to fill the largest halls in the land, yet still make the atmosphere feel like your favourite aunt's front parlour.

It is a relationship grounded in a love for music, and in communicating that love, but it was not a relationship — it must be said — that had its roots in folk music from the beginning. Tony and Mick met at college and their mutual enthusiasm for jazz drew them together.

Neither has lost that zest for his teenage music passion, but at that time, in the mid-1950s, a brief and brilliant diversion was to sweep the nation and give them their first taste of success as well as a healthy boot along the road to fame.

Tony and Mick (both bearded) in their Gin Mill skiffling days at the Cavern

Mick, Tony, Cliff and Jacqui McDonald on one of their 'mad weekend dashes' to London's top 1960's folk venue, the Troubadour

Tony holds the mike for Cliff, watched by Hughie and sister Joan

Hughie with his twelve-stringed guitar, just before his radio debut

There is a Cavern in the town

In the beginning there was Bing and swing, and Vera Lynn, and sweethearts, and the lingering aftertaste of wartime deprivation, rationing and making-do. Popular songs were still sung to the soothing tones of Guy Mitchell or the infectious laughter of Alma Cogan.

But the good times were just beginning to roll, and young kids of the 'You've Never Had It So Good' generation were saying 'Give us a new excitement, give us jubilation, give us a music to rock grannie to her foundation garments.' And skiffle was born.

Skiffle was born in the cradle of jazz, in New Orleans — it was rent party music, born of necessity by impecunious musicians who'd organize a jam session, fill the bathtub with gin, get in the pigs' feet for a feast, charge a dollar at the door — and, after paying for breakages, hope to have made enough bread to survive another week.

British skiffle was born in the mid 1950s of a different necessity. The then current trad jazz boom brought fame to many fine and thirsty bands. Interval time was the signal for the trumpet/trombone/clarinet brigade to head for the orange juice, leaving the stage to maybe the drummer and the strummers, plus the piano player, to fill in time. Out of such necessity came several bonuses. One was Acker Bilk's fine piano player Dave Collett, whose interval improvizations brought Acker his hummable hit Summer Set.

Another was Lonnie Donegan, whose uninhibited banjo style turned skiffle into a national craze. In fact, it was in 1954 that the Chris Barber band made an LP which featured Lonnie's version of 'Rock Island Line', but it was not released as a single until 1956.

Skiffle was loud, brash — and cheap. It could be played on washboard, cowbells, tea-chest and broom-handle bass, even comb and paper. But it was also rooted not only in jazz but in folk. The Donegan repertoire was not new, it was pure American folklore: 'The Battle of New Orleans', 'Cumberland Gap', 'Bring a Little Water, Sylvie'. Not everyone agreed about skiffle. It was harmless fun, but was it art? Pop contemporary Joe Brown, describing his own career in a showbiz reference book in the 1980s, wrote: 'I was a barrow boy, railway fireman and member of a skiffle group before turning to music . . .'

Lonnie might disagree. He certainly had a deeper regard for the songs and a higher regard for his fans than many gave him credit for. 'I didn't like the fan club syndrome,' he says, 'where kids paid half a crown for the privilege of admiring you. I found it sick. But at the same time kids did come round and want to belong in some way.' So Lonnie founded a number of skiffle and folk appreciation clubs around the country, where young skifflers could gather and let off steam, and where those who wanted to could learn to play the guitar, or learn a little more about American jazz and folk.

Tony Davis, whose formative years had been surrounded by music, and who'd discovered jazz at school, enthusiastically embraced this new and vibrant sound, gathering around him like-minded converts to play for fun and a little profit. In the early 1950s, he founded a skiffle group at college in Manchester and, together with his wife Beryl, also got together the Gin Mill skiffle group on Merseyside. Tony regularly crossed the city to play clarinet with the Manchester College of Art Jazz Band (which at that time also included Cephas Howard, later of the Temperance Seven, in its line-up) and, if there had been more jazzmen at teacher training college, he might well have stayed a committed jazz musician. As it was, he took Beryl's guitar to college instead, and taught himself chords. When skiffle caught on, improvization was the order of the day — so Mick Groves was invited to join and handed a washboard — simply because Tony and his college friends lacked a washboard player. He must have felt like the volunteer who'd drawn the short straw . . .

'Mick was keen, but he'd be the first to admit he wasn't a born washboard player,' Tony admits. But Mick had stickability, and having already made the trip along the East Lancs Road most weekends to play jazz with Tony, now found himself doing the same weekend trip to play in the Gin Mill. 'He'd got ambitious by then, and wanted to play the guitar,' Tony adds. 'So I taught him the three chords I'd taught myself, and he took it from there.'

The Gin Mill, in fact, gathered quite a reputation for itself and became firmly established as a favourite group at the Cavern, in Liverpool's Mathew Street, in its pre-Beatle days. Tony, Mick and Beryl (who plucked a cello like a bass) were joined at various times by a number of like-minded enthusiasts, including Copple Davies (banjo), Gerry Grogan (tuba), Colin Whittick (drums), John Wilson (clarinet) and Alastair Wallace (guitar).

With his precise mind and flair for admin, it seemed natural that Mick should also become secretary of the Liverpool branch of Lonnie's club at the Cavern, which at one time even numbered Paul McCartney and George Harrison among its members.

Skiffle was an essential ingredient of the folk revival that was to come. Not a pure strain, it gave the revival a 'pop' edge from the start; not wholly beneficial either, some might say, but ultimately far from harmful. 'Let's face it, the British are not the greatest music lovers,' confesses Lonnie. 'I made it easier for them often, by adapting the lyrics to make them more palatable. But above all, I tried to make it fun.' Lonnie, however, was not the one to lead a folk revival. Fans demanded of him solely the hits that blasted their way into the charts. He became typecast by his own success, and it was left to others to carry the torch for alternative music.

Already the Gin Mill skiffle group had set itself apart

from other Cavern groups, who usually came along and aped whatever was in the charts at the time. The Gin Mill sang some pop, but also interspersed their programme with traditional songs. 'Tony introduced me to Leadbelly and Woody Guthrie,' says Mick, 'and we started broadening our repertoire with the John and Alan Lomax folk collections.'

Neither Tony nor Mick pretend that their experiments were wholly successful. Pioneers before their time, their efforts often met with complete indifference from a Cavern audience eager for Lonnie's latest. Teenagers then tended to react to all 'folk' with the same disdain they reserved for 'classics' taught them by that lingering species, the straight-laced, prim and joyless school music-teacher.

'We took school songs like "A 'Roving", "John Peel", "The Lincolnshire Poacher", and we gave them a new feel with banjo and whistle. They were well-known, but often scorned by the young as a bad memory, so we tried to make them more lively. We knew they were *still* good songs, but — sadly — they mixed with skiffle at the Cavern to disastrous effect,' remembers Tony.

Once Tin Pan Alley had pounced on and packaged the raw skiffle sound into sanitized chart successes, the fun seemed to go out of it somehow. Skiffle groups increasingly found themselves facing two options — either to ride the crest of an uncertain wave and be swallowed up in the great pop and beat revolution that was gathering pace, or retreat to the minority stream of folkies, after only scratching the surface of a rediscovered sound. Interest in folk music was devoted but minimal in Britain at that time. The efforts of the English Folk Dance and Song Society were sincere, and the folk song collections of its founder Cecil Sharp and others had added much to the knowledge of the richness of our folk heritage. But, by and large, enjoyment of folk music was restricted to the nether regions of the Third Programme.

Gradually, however, through new interest in American folk performers such as Burl Ives, Harry Belafonte, the Weavers (with Pete Seeger), the Kingston Trio, and in the songs of Woody Guthrie and Leadbelly, a reawakening began. And, in the backlash against the throbbing headache of rock and roll, an alternative music scene began to emerge. The prime evangelist of this folk revival was Peter Kennedy, whose radio series 'As I Roved Out' brought raw and exciting traditional talents of Britain and Ireland to an eager, if initially startled, audience. Unexpectedly, the seedbed for the folk revival in England was the then staid and starchy BBC. Kennedy's series grew out of a traditional song spot on a Sunday programme called 'Country Magazine'. Folk chroniclers and performers Ewan MacColl and A. L. Lloyd also found radio niches, and wrote definitive studies of this absorbing and largely untapped folk culture of the British Isles. At about the same time John Hasted, a professor of atomic energy at University College London who had started Club 44 in London and ran the London Youth Choir, began to organize folk and skiffle parties, for reasons partly traditional and partly political.

Between them all, they became the princes to reawaken the sleeping beauty of folk music.

The green baize faithful

The Gin Mill was the first really successful outfit Tony, Mick and Beryl were associated with. Not only were they playing regular dates at clubs and hotels and the Cavern, but they appeared at the Liverpool Empire on the same bill as Michael Holliday and the Squadronaires, and at the Manchester Hippodrome with the Sid Phillips Band, as well as doing interval spots with Mick Mulligan's jazz band and others.

But it was the Cavern which provided their regular audience, every Wednesday night. The Gin Mill became Cavern residents, and other skiffle groups — such as John Lennon's Quarrymen — would come and do their guest spots.

The Cavern was a great nursery for all kinds of musical expression, and when the scene started going electric at the birth of Merseybeat — and Beatlemania — Tony and Mick decided it was time to pack it in. They had ridden the jazz and skiffle express as far as they wanted to go. Neither of them was interested in being just another pop group, so now they sought a new platform for their talents, having reached one of the first 'make your mind up' points of their careers. 'The music press were saying, "Skiffle is dead",' says Mick, 'and we used to say, "They must be crackers!" You could open the *Liverpool Echo* any night and find dozens of groups advertised in venues scattered all over Merseyside. But eventually the scene started to split, and we found ourselves having to decide which way we wanted to go.'

Realizing the dawn of a new music age was upon them, they pondered a future as singers of folk songs. 'The trouble was, the only folk performers we knew at that time were singing solid Ewan MacColl stuff in Ewan MacColl style, and I knew I didn't want to become another Ewan MacColl,' explains Mick. And so, eager to find their own expression of folk, and stamp their inimitable mark on the new scene, Tony and Mick decided to explore the folk phenomenon from the beginning. And in their back to basics search, they sought out the local branch of the English Folk Dance and Song Society.

Flipping through the pages of the telephone book they discovered that its members met on the third Wednesday of each month in the Friends' Meeting House; they went along, and it wasn't at all what they had expected. 'We stumbled on a whole crowd of very nice people, sitting around a green baize table — the ladies still wearing their coats and with their Sunday-best hats on, and the gentlemen in suits — with these erudite tomes open in front of them,' remembers Tony. It was certainly a religious setting and atmosphere for the revival that was to come. 'We were introduced to an evening of "sea chanties",' Tony went on, ' and the man leading the singing gave them the note and said, "Right, ladies, all together now . . . 'Way hay, and up she rises' ", and they all joined in, doing their very best. We looked at each other and thought, "What have we unearthed?" But they were kind, and they had an undeniable fervour, a passion for what they were doing. So we stuck with them.

'The next month they explored variants of "Edward, My Son", the week after that it was rounds. It wasn't at all what we'd expected it to be, and we quickly learnt to hide our guitars in the corner, because obviously that wasn't what they wanted at all. We were also at a disadvantage, as we couldn't read music. They were, however, obviously devout about what they were doing. Folk music had got to them — it was in their bowels. Only they had been brought up to sing it genteelly, and to articulate nicely.'

Feeling they had something to give this group, as well as to take from it, Tony and Mick one week introduced them to Red Sullivan, an ex-ship's stoker who was deeply into the folk traditions of Britain and America (and even sang blues) — yet with just a little more feeling. When he sang 'sea chanties' to the green baize table club, it was with a depth of interpretation which moved one lady to remark: 'We may sing these songs, and enjoy singing them, but this man — he's *lived* them!'

Tony and Mick determined to continue their homework, exploring the potential of folk through the Society. Then, in May 1958, came a chance to try their new-found sound on a wider weekend audience. Tony's father had been approached to see if the Gin Mill was still in operation and could provide the music for a Conservative Party fête on Aigburth cricket ground in Liverpool. That their first gig should be a Tory fête is an historical fact that has become a source of much embarrassment and amusement over the years, bearing in mind the causes the Spinners have since supported; but Tony's father, having tentatively committed them, suggested they 'go along and do something'.

The Gin Mill had by then been disbanded for some six months, but memories lingered, and Tony warned his father and the organizers that it would be a totally different musical experience. He rounded up Beryl, and Mick brought along his fiancée Margaret, and Stan Francis, a draughtsman and ship's engineer whom they'd met at Lonnie Donegan nights at the Cavern. It was the only time Margaret, a more than reluctant recruit, was to sing with them ('Which was such a pity, as she had a really sweet voice,' says Tony), and initial qualms about accepting the date were quelled by a generous and pleasing reception. So much so, that people began asking where they could hear them regularly.

They therefore went in search of a new city club as a base — and a name.

Such is the group feeling among the Spinners that none of them is totally sure who first coined the name. Certainly, when they were asked to play at Aigburth, they needed a folksy name that would reflect their new style, and one that would reflect the working traditions of Lancashire maybe . . . in the end, 'The Spinners' seemed to evolve and the Gin Mill was no more.

Their first venue was found in the basement of Samson and Barlow's restaurant in Liverpool's London Road. Smaller than the Cavern, it would take forty at a sweaty push, but it was cosy and it was a good testing ground. The boys opened their club on a Friday night in September 1958, and that same evening caught the overnight London bus from St Johns Lane, Liverpool, to appear at the Royal Festival Hall in their first English Folk Dance and Song Society jamboree.

In fact, they closed the proceedings, singing 'Roll, Bullies, Roll', on stage with a very mixed cast — there was Harry Boardman, the senior north-west folk pioneer and a diehard of the MacColl school, John Hasted's Choir, and the Ranchers, a band of mostly young public-school types (very EFDSS at that time). Each collected a certificate to say they were now 'certified folk singers'.

The Spinners had truly been born, and from then on, they never looked back.

Mick

'Fried bread and brandy-o,
On a fine spring morning-o,
If I had someone to choose,
I'd choose my mighty Mickey-o.'

Mick Groves was born in the 'dirty old town' of Salford. Always keen on singing, his first musical experiences were with the Catholic church when he became an altar boy. From church music he moved on to campfire sing-alongs with the Scouts and eventually an E-flat euphonium in a Scout band.

'My family were not that musical — my mother's family had a piano and one of her brothers played an accordion, but this euphonium was the first instrument I had actually been asked to play. I just had to follow sheets of music that basically told me what valve to press and when. Obviously, it was the wrong way to learn, and it didn't last very long — but it was interesting . . .' he remembers.

Always eager to try new experiences, he would get up at youth club dances and ape the latest hit of singers like Frankie Laine or Guy Mitchell, but it wasn't until he went to college that he found music he could identify with — jazz. 'I'd listened to the Saints Jazz Band before I went to college — but always from outside the Grosvenor House Hotel in Manchester because I was too young and too scruffy to go inside. Then, when I got to college, I asked who I had to see about joining the jazz group — and that's how I got introduced to Tony.'

That meeting at teacher training college was to establish a long-term friendship and began frequent trips to Merseyside to play weekends at the West Coast Jazz Club.

'I used to come and spend the weekend at Tony's mum's in Wallasey, and that was a great thrill for me, as it meant I could see the sea. The seaside was always a big thing for Salford kids in those days — it was generally where you went for your holidays, and to contemplate actually *living* near the sea was — to me — quite amazing. To walk along the beach each morning was out of this world.'

Mick also found the music scene more vibrant in Liverpool than in Manchester; but neither his father, a labourer on a building site, nor his mother was keen on him moving. ' "Out of the frying pan into the fire," they said' — but it was a move Mick made early, and with no regrets. His only enduring link with his native city these days — apart from those members of his family who still live there — is a continuing and absorbing passion for Manchester United FC.

'Tony sported a big red beard in those days, and I didn't really grow until I was in my twenties — and then not very much — so we must have looked like David and Goliath,' Mick remembers. 'But I'd found a soul brother, and we played jazz, and we played skiffle together, and together we learnt a lot.' Maybe as an 'if you can't beat 'em, join 'em' gesture, Mick grew a natty Van Dyke beard in his days at the Cavern. It soon disappeared, however.

The Gin Mill had a varied and interesting repertoire: Tony was keen on Ken Colyer jazz, American folk and blues, while Mick specialized more in the pop scene and in Lonnie's inspired chartbusters. By this time they were alternating at the Cavern with the Ron Mackay Skiffle Group and laying the foundation for the big Merseybeat revolution that was to come.

All those who played the Cavern seem to have their own memories of outrageous happening and fun events — Mick remembers celebrating his twenty-first birthday there, when his family hired a double-decker bus from Manchester and drove over one Sunday lunchtime to park it in Mathew Street and join in the party. 'We were doing Sunday lunchtimes with the Royal Caribbean Serenaders, and Clinton Ford — who was then singing with the Merseysippi Band — doing a solo spot, when suddenly this bus rolls up and stops outside. I couldn't believe it.'

The Cavern was not licensed and had only a soft drinks bar, but the group had managed to smuggle in some crates of beer and bottles of spirits. 'So members of the family were going up to the bar during the afternoon and saying, "I'm with Mick Groves' party" (wink, nudge, say no more) "Can I have a Coke?" and getting liberally dosed with whatever . . .'

Not content with throwing central Liverpool into confusion, Beryl then proceeded to invite the whole party back to the Davis' home in Thirlmere Drive, Wallasey, for tea! So the same double-decker bus went through the Tunnel and threaded its way into this little Wirral cul-de-sac as well.

'By this time I was feeling quite ill — I think I was sickening for flu or something anyway — so I went upstairs to lie down in the box room. And people were coming in and throwing their coats on the bed before going down to tuck into the cakes and food Beryl had prepared. I was sweating it out upstairs while they were drinking my health downstairs. It was a crazy, memorable, occasion.'

Tony and Mick eventually (and surprisingly) graduated as teachers and Mick got a job at Westminster Road Catholic Boys' School before transferring to All Souls, off Liverpool's notorious Scotland Road.

'All Souls was an amazing school, straight out of Dickens, with open fires, a playground no bigger than the average lounge, outside toilets (and it was a mixed school). The headmaster's office had a real Dickens desk and chair, situated between what was really just two classrooms, with no partitions, so you had a teacher operating either side of the headmaster. It was unbelievably ancient but the kids were great.

'They were mostly from the tenements that surrounded the school (just down from where Cilla Black was born) and after school and at weekends they used to play football in the courts between the tenements. One Friday when I was on playground duty, the kids came to me and said: "Look sir, they're ruining our footy pitch" — and I saw council workmen putting in concrete posts to section off the court for the residents.

'Now the residents didn't mind the kids playing football the length of the court, but the council in its wisdom had decided to section it off and give each tenement its own patch. So I said in my innocence: 'Well there's not a lot you can do about it, is there ?" I should have known better. Come the Monday the kids came up to me and said: "We got our footy pitch back, sir." I looked again and all these concrete posts were flattened. The kids had spent the whole weekend rocking them back and forth till they collapsed.

'It was, if you like, my first understanding of inner-city attitudes. Anyone else coming along would have said, "Ruddy vandals" — but to the kids it was justified. No one had asked them if they minded losing their footy pitch. No one had thought, "Here's a large and useful play area. Let's leave well enough alone." The kids hadn't been vicious in their action — they had just taken positive steps to get what they wanted, and they'd succeeded.'

His time at All Souls stood Mick in good stead when he went, as a science teacher, to St Gregory's — a new secondary school in the same area. Although it was a rough, tough environment, he found himself protected virtually by his own praetorian guard, the lads he had taught and impressed when they were seven. Other teachers were surprised by the influence he had over the biggest tearaways in the school, but it was only because he had done his groundwork at All Souls.

'The older pupils at St Gregory's used to go down the Cavern every lunchtime and, at the end of term, they asked if they could hold a school dance. They booked the Searchers and I had to stand behind them in this, and encourage them against one or two other teachers who weren't keen on the idea at all. It didn't help allay their fears when the Searchers turned up, because they — like the Beatles — had recently been to Hamburg, and they were dressed all in black leather, looking scruffy as hell — such was the fashion among rock bands in those days.

'What a night it was! It didn't end in disaster but it kept everyone on their toes and it certainly rocked the old establishment.'

Finally Mick rose to become acting head of science at the respected St Francis Xavier School, next to the church where he was married, but by then the Spinners were getting so big that it was time to make a decision that would affect his life and his future . . .

'We were doing incredibly stupid things like travelling to London on Friday nights and travelling back overnight on Sundays to go to work the next day. It was good fun meeting people like Ewan MacColl, Dominic Behan, Alexis Korner, Long John Baldry, Red Sullivan . . . and sleeping on people's floors for a couple of nights, singing in the Troubadour till all hours, but it was a punishing, demanding schedule.

'By the end of my first year at St Francis Xavier I was given the opportunity to plan the new science labs. It was interesting work and my headmaster hinted also that he was in a position to offer another £140 a year . . . and that was a lot of money then. So it was — as they say — make your mind up time.'

If the thought of turning professional and earning their money at music scared the boys, it shocked their wives. Mick's wife Margaret says, 'I married a schoolteacher, and there was no reason to think he'd remain anything other than a schoolteacher.' She had met Mick at the Cavern in the Gin Mill days and accepted that Mick enjoyed singing as a release from the rigours of the classroom. They were married at St Francis Xavier's church in Liverpool, and when the Spinners eventually went professional, she was expecting the first of their four children. They now have three boys, Michael, Matthew and David, and a girl, Lisa.

'We had the three boys in three years and I won't pretend I didn't find it difficult during those early years with Mick away so much with the group. But it got easier as they got older, and it's a way of life you get used to.'

As the group became better known, and didn't necessarily

have to take every job which came their way, Mick found himself home more regularly and able to see more of his growing family. 'The Spinners always made it a rule to have the school holidays at home,' explains Margaret, 'so the children probably saw as much of him as if he'd stayed a schoolteacher.'

In Samson and Barlow days Margaret had been a club regular; she ran the door and kept the club books for two years and then became secretary/bookkeeper for four years or more. But the very first Spinners' outing to that Aigburth fête she prefers to forget. 'I think they're being very kind when they say I had a nice voice. I was gripped with fear and embarrassment!'

Later she immersed herself in her family, and developed her talents as an actress in local amateur dramatic roles with the St Alban's Players, yet she still remains an essentially private person. Family life is obviously important to the Spinners, and to the Groveses in particular. Their home is a welcome retreat from the pressures of performing and the public.

Tony

'Fried bread and brandy-o
On a summer's morning-o,
If I had someone to choose,
I'd choose my tiny Tony-o.'

Six foot seven inches (or two metres for metricated readers) of sore and tender Tony stretched out on a barely adequate bed in Wrightington Hospital, Lancashire, naked save for a blue aertex blanket. It was June 1981.

He had been in for a hip replacement operation to correct a complaint which had troubled him since he was thrown by a pony when he was seven, and which had grown progressively more painful over the years. He had gone into the Army in his late teens with thoughts of becoming a regular officer, but this recurring osteo-arthritis meant he'd been invalided out after fifteen months. Now the pain had finally gone, and agony and apprehension were replaced by admiration for the skill of the surgeons and the sheer relief of it all.

The room was filled with get-well cards, fruit, flowers — and music, while Tony talked ceaselessly about anything and everything and in a tone that could be heard two wards away.

Requests by the nurses to take it easy and please be quiet were noted with contrition and then forgotten in his eagerness and enthusiasm for the conversation in hand. Wrightington could seldom have had a more vociferous,

The Spinners and families, as they appeared on the cover of their 1966 Family of Man *album*

Meeting heroes: Brownie McGhee, Cliff, Sonny Terry and happy club members at the Cavern in 1968

Dance 'n' Skylark – rehearsing with Stan Hugill for their first major television series in Manchester

vibrant, or grateful patient. But top-gear living comes naturally to Tony — he is never a man to stay in neutral for long.

If over the years he has refuted all suggestions that he is 'leader' of the Spinners (they are strictly a democratic cooperative, all decisions taken jointly) he is nevertheless their powerhouse, their energy source from which the others perhaps find inspiration, certainly find encouragement. Tony is a man who gets things and people moving. His sister Joan, who sang with the Spinners in the very early days, described him as a 'man who gets people involved — a great chucker-in at the deep end'.

For instance, she and Tony's other sister Wendy would be press-ganged at college into giving lectures to the jazz club, armed with a script from Tony and the relevant LPs; and only when they found themselves at the front of a group of eager, expectant people would they suddenly think: 'What on earth am I doing here!' And their own ingenuity would be stretched to snapping point come question time, when they sank or swam by using their wits — and Tony was nowhere to be found.

Tony was in fact born in Blackburn, but left with his family to move to Merseyside when he was three. He naturally remembers little of his Lancashire childhood except those tales handed down as family legends — like the time he went missing at a tender age, and only after the local police had dragged the canal and the ditches was he found in the coalhouse, nibbling the coal. Or the time a neighbour kidded him that the three taps in his kitchen were for hot water, cold water and lemonade — and he believed it.

Tony's father was a Man from the Pru who rose to become an insurance inspector, and took his family to live in various parts of Merseyside before settling on the Wirral. He died in his fifties of cancer.

It was a fragmented childhood for Tony, punctuated by the war which meant enforced moves to Benllech on Anglesey and later to Kendal on the edge of Lakeland. Education was completed at Wallasey Grammar School; and it was here that Tony got hooked on jazz and started to play the clarinet after being a prime mover in setting up the school's jazz appreciation society.

Music had been an essential part of growing up, anyway. His grandmother he remembers singing Irish music-hall songs round the house, the old Jimmy O'Dea favourites. And whenever the family went for outings in his father's car they would sing as they travelled, mostly the pop tunes of the 1930s. Tony couldn't play an instrument in those days, though he might pick out a tune with one finger on his grandparents' piano, nor could he read music.

But the clarinet entranced him — after listening to the early Mugsy Spanier recording of 'I Wish I Could Shimmy Like My Sister Kate' with a vocal by George Brunis, backed by a piece called 'Eccentric' which had a marvellous clarinet solo by Rod Cless.

'I still think the clarinet is the most superb instrument, especially for jazz, and I enjoy listening to all the greats from Johnny Dodds and Sidney Bechet through Benny Goodman to Acker Bilk. It's a very beautiful instrument, though a bit loud for a folk group so I compromise by playing the whistle. Cliff Hall would now probably say that's just as well . . . "Piercing, man" is his usual comment when I go over the top.'

Jazz is still Tony's greatest hobby — alongside sailing. He'll go and listen when he's free to either the Blue Magnolia Jass Orchestra ('a very entertaining band') or the Merseysippis, the two big Liverpool outfits. 'They might get me up to sing or fool around on the kazoo or something, just for the hell of it.'

Long before the Spinners, Tony had his own jazz group, variously called the Rivington Ramblers (after the road he lived in) or the Storyville Stompers (shades of New Orleans) or eventually the Muskrat Jazz Band.

He had a way of recruiting personnel which took precedence even over romance. When he was courting Beryl (now his wife) he once walked her home, only to hear the strains of the family's piano wafting from the front room. As his band was desperate for a piano player at the time, he rushed in and offered Beryl's sister Muriel the job — oblivious of the fact that Beryl could play just as well.

But it was Muriel who was taught how to vamp, and to forget how to read music, with the Muskrats.

It was during a spell with the British American Tobacco company in Liverpool — one of a number of uninspiring office jobs he tried before entering college — that Tony had met Beryl. They were both in the factory swimming team and went together to compete in a London festival. Before too long they found themselves taking another plunge — they celebrated their Silver Wedding in 1981; and have two daughters, Susan and Jackie. Their whole marriage has been the Spinners, and neither of them look on a moment of it as wasted. In fact, jazz was to permeate their honeymoon too. Having arrived in Paris, and relaxing in a Left Bank bistro, Tony and Beryl were introduced to Albert Nicholas, then an elderly man, but at one time a New Orleans pioneer with the original King Oliver band.

'We had a great time listening to his memories, drinking with him, laughing, singing, and eventually he invited us back to his place. He was a little the worse for wear then, and so were we, and when we got there he collapsed on the bed. We didn't like to leave him, so we collapsed on the floor. It was a fun night and we followed it up by sending postcards to our friends telling them we'd spent the first night of our honeymoon with Albert Nicholas. Those who knew would be impressed — those who didn't would just wonder . . .'

Beryl — who freely admits that if Tony tells her to do something she's willing to have a go, and who has been a faithful victim of being 'chucked in at the deep end' over the years — played banjo in Tony's jazz group, guitar and cello with the Gin Mill, piano for her own amusement and in recent years has taken up the accordion, teaching herself how to play each instrument.

What is Beryl's attitude to the Spinners' success and to her husband's part in it?

'When I see him on stage doing his act, he's not the same person I know when he walks off — none of them is. On stage he's a performer, but when he walks off he's Tony Davis, not a Spinner, and I expect him to be a natural person, not putting on an act. If anyone recognizes him I expect him to treat them as if he was Tony Davis; the fact that he's a Spinner is not something which makes him better than them. But it does mean he has a double responsibility, if you like, to be extra decent.

'We've been married twenty-five years, and in reality all our marriage has been the Spinners, but I don't feel I've lived my life in the limelight. I have a fond belief nobody knows who I am — now and again I realize that isn't true.'

Tony's height (which is a family characteristic) has always been a source of amazement and amusement. At one time, Jacqui McDonald, who made contact with the Spinners when she came to Liverpool to attend college and became a regular with the group for more than three years, drove a bubble car. Minis were fresh on the scene about this time, and whereas Tony found it difficult to get his lanky frame inside the conventional layout of a Mini, he could easily get in and out of the bubble, with its wide front-opening door. 'It always drew a gasp at the Mersey Tunnel entrance when Tony unfolded himself from my passenger seat to pay the man in the toll booth,' Jacqui recalls.

Tony was also the slowest eater she knew. 'We would pick him up in the van and he would come out with maybe a slice of toast still in his hand, not having finished his breakfast, and that toast seemed to last him until we got to Birmingham. Mind you, he would also be talking a fair amount of the way.

'Then, when we'd finished and arrived home at maybe five in the morning, he'd tuck into a bowl of cornflakes before going to bed . . .'

The Spinners' line-up wasn't perfect when they first opened their club at Samson and Barlow's ('We were a gang which became a group,' explains Tony's sister Joan) — and so Tony went in search of the man he believed could give the emerging group an extra ingredient, to give the Spinners' sound a unique and captivating flavour.

Tony wasn't a natural office worker — he much preferred being out of doors, and while clerking at the Atomic Energy site at Capenhurst in 1953 (before he went to college) he had discovered that he could earn twice as much if he got his hands dirty labouring — so he did. But he had been in the office one day when an electrician working on the site was called to fix a fault. His name was Cliff Hall.

'I walked into the office and said to the guy behind the desk (that was Tony), "What's the trouble?" And he said, "I'll show you"... and he got up — and up! Man, I'd never seen anybody that tall in my life before!' remembers Cliff.

Tony explains: 'I confess I was going through a very heavy "black is beautiful" period. I was a jazz nut, and to me negroes were gods. Negro blues singers and Van Gogh's paintings are the only two things in life that have made me cry instinctively. Mahalia Jackson singing 'The Last Mile of the Way" made me weep the first time I heard it. Negro singers were just something else . . . but I didn't know any black people till I met Cliff at Capenhurst. So I sought him out after our first meeting. I thought, "He's black. He's bound to know about music." It seemed inconceivable that he wouldn't at least know calypsoes.'

But Cliff was suspicious of this tall white stranger tailing him. The only other white men who had shown that much interest in him had been politically motivated ultra-lefties of the Electrical Trades Union, and Cliff, who is not at all a political person, didn't want to know. And, although he had been brought up in the rich and vibrant musical tradition of the Caribbean, he wasn't particularly interested in music at this time. But Tony refused to believe that any black person could be indifferent to rhythm. To him black was magic; it meant excitement, jazz and blues. It was impossible that Cliff shouldn't have music in his soul.

'He kept on wanting to talk to me, and I kept on being cautious of him, until one day I said, "Listen, man, don't be too friendly. It's people like you that do more damage by forcing yourself on us than those who abuse us. So take it easy . . ."' Eventually, however, some sort of mutual understanding sprang up between the two men, firmly cemented when Tony found out that Cliff had a guitar and was turned on by country music, purely for his own amusement.

'You have to remember that, at that time,' explains Tony, 'Jamaicans in this country were interested in any form of music except their own. West Indian music meant back home, maybe a spot of home-sickness, maybe memories of poverty and slavery.'

Tony did, however, lose touch with Cliff when he went to college, and his weekends were full of other things; but several years on, when the Spinners began to get a following at Samson and Barlow's, Tony went walking the streets of Liverpool 8, the city area where Cliff lived, seeking him in the hope of luring him back to those childhood Jamaican rhythms.

Cliff

'Fried bread and brandy-o,
On an autumn morning-o,
If I had someone to choose,
I'd choose my lanky Cliffy-o.'

We were sitting round a restaurant table in Liverpool's Chinatown, chatting about a concert the Spinners had just done in the city's Bluecoat Chambers, when two Geordie girls came over.

'You're the Spinners, aren't you?' one of them said.

Tony agreed.

'I wouldn't have known, only my friend here recognized him,' she added, pointing at Cliff.

'Must be the moustache,' said Tony, as they signed their names.

If Cliff is the maverick in the Spinners set-up, he is also their master-stroke. From its beginnings in the late 1950s he set the group apart from its contemporaries, a more eloquent statement on racial harmony than any protest song, and at a time when such things as equality, tolerance and brotherhood were barely fashionable.

But more than that, he brought the Spinners an undeniable Caribbean flavour, a Jamaican spice to add to a very English recipe.

Cliff Hall was born in Cuba of Jamaican parents, who moved back to their native island in 1939 when war broke out. Cliff had started school in Cuba, learning Spanish and

English. His mother died and his father married again. Times were hard in the Caribbean and when Cliff went with his father and family back to Jamaica, he left school to work in the fields. If he had no ambitions for himself, his father certainly felt he could do better, so he sent the young Cliff into Kingston to learn a trade and earn more money.

'My father told me to be careful in the city. "You never know who you might get mixed up with," he would say. He wasn't very strict with me, but he was cautious, and he taught me to have respect for people.'

In Kingston, Cliff got a job moulding breeze blocks for the building industry. 'I just asked this chap on the building site if I could have a job and he said "Yes". So I was humping these blocks around and stacking them for him, then at the end of the week when I went up for my wages, he had gone. I never saw him again. So I thought, this must be what my old man has been warning me about.'

On the edge of town, however, he got pally with a fellow who delivered milk and Cliff joined the farm, milking cows for eighteen months. 'I knew them all one by one. They were just like children. I'd sit there milking and say "Thank you very much. Next one please." '

Cliff had resolved to spend some time in Jamaica getting some money together, then set off and see the world. The RAF was recruiting in Jamaica, so in 1942 he applied, was accepted and came to England. 'That was my first glimpse of snow. We landed in Glasgow on a crisp November evening, beautiful but cold. I was eighteen then, and I was taken to Filey, East Yorkshire, to the training camp, with the rest of the lads. Next morning I woke up and there was all this white dust blowing about — I was amazed and called the other lads to see it. Then we went out and started playing in it. Next day I was crippled with chilblains — nobody had warned me about that!'

Quite a number of young Jamaicans came over with Cliff, and for all of them it was a new experience. Eventually they were dispersed over the country and Cliff went to the RAF maintenance unit at Hartlebury in Worcestershire, where he made a lot of English friends. In fact, by the time he'd been in England two and a half years and had travelled around with the RAF collecting and delivering aircraft parts, he had met a Scottish lass called Janet, fallen in love and decided to stay in England.

'I met her in Leeds before I got my demob. I had been sent there on an electrical course, and we decided to get married four days before I was due to go back to Jamaica.'

That was in 1947, five years after he had volunteered for the RAF. His homecoming could have been traumatic but in fact it was full of understanding and affection. 'My father and my family were delighted for me. There was no pressure put on me to stay in Jamaica — it was my life and as long as I was happy and looked after myself, they were content.'

So Cliff came back to England in 1948, got a job with an electrical contractor and stayed. The early 1950s were exciting years — there was a feeling of rebirth in the air, people were seeking new experiences, everything was a challenge, and the music reflected the age of optimism.

Cliff got hooked on a sound he'd picked up on his wireless from the American Forces Network. He bought himself a big black guitar and strummed along with his favourites — Jimmy Rogers, Hank Williams — for his own amusement. The music of Jamaica all but forgotten, he immersed himself in becoming country and westernized.

It was during this period of adjustment that he met Tony at Capenhurst in 1953.

After the shaky start, Tony and Cliff eventually got on to the same wavelength and became firm friends, Cliff agreeing to come to Liverpool and hear Tony's jazz group play.

'He took me to a pub up the London Road near to the Royal Infirmary, and during the evening I wanted some pennies to make a phone-call. So I took a sixpence from my pocket and went over to the barman to ask for change. Between me and the bar was this big Alsatian belonging to the landlord, and he had a bone in his mouth. I didn't notice that at first, and bent over to pat the dog. As I did so he sank his teeth into my hand!

'It was lucky we were so close to the Infirmary — I

quickly went there, had an injection and my hand bandaged. Everyone was very apologetic back at the pub — but what a welcome!'

Even after that episode their friendship blossomed, and the West Indian found himself another victim of Tony's habit of chucking people in at the deep end.

Tony's jazz group at that time was an eight-piece but to fulfil the contract for a New Year date in Wallasey had to be increased to a twelve-piece for one night only. Cliff was cajoled into beating bongo drums that evening — all he had to do was look good and collect his fee.

Tony was following a hunch when he went seeking Cliff again after several years of separation. Fortunately Cliff wasn't that hard to track down, and this time the Jamaican songs of his childhood and those Jamaican rhythms seemed to come more easily, instinctively, naturally.

'I only knew one song then, but over the months snatches of others I had known in my youth started to come back to me. Songs I hadn't sung since my childhood but which were stored in my memory would come to me maybe while I was in bed, and I'd get up in the morning and write the words down before they went again,' says Cliff.

'Cliff could play rhythm on the guitar like it had always been there,' Tony recalls. 'He had two distinctive licks — one fast, one slow — and they were totally different, not only from each other but from anything we had heard before. It wasn't a tango, or a rumba, or a calypso, but a more gentle, more subtle, Jamaican rhythm. It was years before the others caught on to how he did it. We had Jimmy McGregor at the club watching Cliff and listening to him and saying "Do that again . . . and again . . ." as he tried to pick it up.'

Surrounded by the encouraging atmosphere and friendship of Samson and Barlow's, Cliff blossomed. But his family needed more convincing that their son was going to be a folk entertainer. Laughter rocked the old homestead when he said he was going to be a professional singer and musician — but that laughter quickly turned to pride as Cliff improved under his own dogged perseverance.

'The first time I went back to Jamaica after joining the

Spinners was in 1968. My parents knew I was in the entertainment business, and they knew I was singing, though I don't think they really believed it — until one day the Spinners were played on their radio and there I was. I didn't go around telling everybody what I was doing. I figured so long as it wasn't anything bad, they'd hear about it sooner or later. And when they did, my old man was made up — really delighted — with it. So when I went back to Kingston I found myself in demand for interviews on JBC, and everybody wanted to know how come I was making a living out of singing when I hadn't shown any inclination for it in my youth. And I used to tell them, "It's as much a puzzle to me as it is to you." '

Cliff grew bolder, and eventually decided to take up the harmonica too. 'I was very bad at it to start with, and my wife, who is normally very patient, was driven on several occasions to shout: "If you don't stop that racket, I'm going to leave you!" But I remember saying to her, "One day you're going to be glad I'm doing this, because I'm going to earn my living playing these instruments." Mind you, I don't think I believed what I was saying was gospel . . .'

His wife Janet had firm views on Cliff's ideas of becoming a performer. 'I thought we'd all starve to death,' she says in her direct Scottish way.

Janet comes from a village between Glasgow and Hamilton, and in those days had a reputation for being quick-tempered — 'Though you wouldn't think it to see me now,' she says, smiling. But if she wasn't keen on Cliff giving up his electrician's job and becoming a Spinner, she reconciled herself to it in typical Scottish fashion. 'The extra money would come in handy, I thought.'

Cliff and Janet have now been married for over thirty-five years and have three children — Lynne, Clifford and Robert. So what were her parents' reactions to her marrying a West Indian? 'My mother wasn't keen, but I got married before I told her . . . My daddy didn't mind and, anyway, when Cliff met the family, he completely won them over.'

Theirs is an obviously affectionate marriage — Cliff is placid, loves tinkering with his cars and pottering in the garden. Janet, too, used to go to the club but does not go so often now. 'We're both taking it easier now,' she insists. 'We haven't had a bad life really.'

From indifferent beginnings Cliff's music and singing has developed over the years until it is identifiable as his own unique sound. 'I didn't set out to copy anybody. Just be myself. I figured it out from the start that if I tried to copy other performers and do a song their way I would lose the essence of the song. I might even like the way they do it but my interpretation had to be slightly different. It had to be me.

'And, of course, if you're interested in what you're doing, you'll enjoy yourself, and other people will see you enjoying yourself and relax and enjoy themselves too. That repartee between the audience and us is like we're sitting down there with them. We feel they're part of us and that's the way it should be.'

Cliff has been beneficial to the group — 'We used to joke and say he brought a little colour into our lives — but it was true,' says Mick. 'We could have been any other folk group singing traditional songs. Cliff brought that Caribbean quality that gave us a sound which marked us apart from other groups on the scene.' Added to that was Cliff's fine harmonica playing; he has evolved his own inimitable style, playing it very much like an English concertina — an incredible sound. His voice is naturally soft, with a pleasing Caribbean lilt to it that complements not only the more strident tones of Hughie but also the harsher northern accents around him.

Cliff's repertoire and reputation grew at Samson and Barlow's basement, where the Spinners performed to their growing number of fans each Friday evening. But he, like the others, was always looking for fresh talent among the audience, encouraging floor singers to get up and do their own thing, nurturing what has always been their trademark and their great contribution to the folk movement — audience participation.

'We were singing in Samson and Barlow,' said Cliff, 'and

we used to see Hughie come in and hide his guitar in the corner, and sit there all scared and shy. So one day we said to him, "Hey, why not show us you can play that thing?" So he did, and he was good.

'Stan Francis was still with us then, but he wanted to leave and concentrate on making guitars. So Tony asked Hughie to join us, and he was made up.'

Hughie

'Fried bread and brandy-o
On a winter's morning-o
If I had someone to choose
I'd choose my handsome Hughie-o.'

It seemed decreed by fate that Hughie Jones should be an entertainer — there was always more than a slight strain of extrovert eccentricity in his upbringing, notably instilled by his father, who was a tango dance champion and a professional baseball player among other things.

'Anything but work,' remembers Hughie. 'He was completely wild. Money just swept through his hands.'

Hughie is in fact the only born and bred Scouser of the Spinners, born in 1936 in the south end of the city to a Welsh-speaking father and an English piano-teacher mother. His father was the son of Hugh Jones, a very successful Welsh builder who died leaving a small fortune. With his portion of the inheritance, Hughie's father married and took his bride on honeymoon to London.

He did his time as a parquet floor layer, a tiler and a joiner, solid apprenticeships for a life in the trade. 'But he was a dilettante, and he used to keep very bad company. Boxers and bouncers and the like.'

He also developed a taste for the United States and set sail with £5 and a ticket to make his fortune. The fact that his joiner's tools were lost on the passage worried him not at all, and he seems to have worked his way across America and into Canada, leading a nomadic cowboy existence, before returning to England, so the story goes, with a couple of Indian stock ponies which were sold to Lord Derby's estate for breeding and polo.

After that he played baseball for Manchester under the name Tex Martin before returning to the trade he'd grown up in.

'The boys remember him well,' says Hughie, 'because he used to come to the club and relate his adventures to anyone who would listen.' In the beatnik era he even made himself a joiner's set of beatnik beads out of nuts and bolts and washers. He eventually died of heart trouble, when he was sixty-three.

If his father put the unconventional touches into Hughie's make-up it was his mother who instilled a love of music. 'But she never taught me the piano. I'm afraid I was always too idle to learn. There was always too much else to do that was more interesting — like playing football or something.'

He was thirteen years old when he started learning the guitar, beginning with three chords shown him by a friend called Pete Hayes in the Scouts. Folk Songs attracted him in those days, and especially the simple style of Burl Ives. 'I guess I taught myself to play by copying everything he put on record,' says Hughie. 'I certainly bought all his records.'

By the time he was seventeen Hughie was in a local skiffle group — 'Not of such eminence as the Gin Mill. We never played the Cavern. We called ourselves the High Society Skiffle Group and played the better class of dates — tennis clubs and suchlike.'

In those days there were a lot of good quality guitars in Liverpool. Sailors used to bring them back from the States: American Gibsons which were solid, loud, powerful — just the thing for banging out skiffle. Hughie, however, whose taste had now broadened to take in American blues and who was turned on by the sounds of Leadbelly, decided to convert an old six-string Spanish guitar into a twelve-string blues guitar . . . 'Not really realizing how much pressure you can put on the arm of a twelve-string when they're tightened up. I played it for over a year but gradually the arm started to bow and it became more and more difficult to play as the strings got farther away from the fingerboard.'

Then a blues package came on tour to Liverpool, playing the Mardi Gras at the bottom of Mount Pleasant, and Hughie went along with a harmonica-playing pal called Leon, to hear their idols — Muddy Waters, Sonny Terry and Brownie McGhee. (Unknown to either of them at the time, Tony and Mick were also at the same blues night.)

'It was tremendous, of course,' remembers Hughie, 'and I'll never forget, after the show, going up to Muddy and Sonny and asking for autographs. I've kept those autographs, for that concert really was an important landmark for me.' On the way home from the Mardi Gras by bus, Hughie and Leon were talking excitedly about what they'd just seen and heard, and a chap sitting in the next seat joined in their conversation.

'If you like that sort of blues and folk music,' he told them, 'you ought to go down to the Spinners Club in Samson and Barlow's — if you take your guitar along, you'll even get in free!' (That chap's name was Dan Dare. Still remembered around the Liverpool club scene, he was a university lecturer and a motor-bike freak, and an aspiring Spanish guitar player.)

So Hughie took his advice. 'The first week I went, I hid the guitar in the corner, because I was too shy to do anything else and it was such a new experience. I had always associated performing with theatre where you're seemingly miles away from the action — but this was live music only six feet or so in front of you. You could touch those who were singing if you had a mind to — it was all very strange.' He was not very impressed with what he heard. 'They weren't really a group — just a collection of singers. One would sing a song and if the others knew the chorus, they would join in.'

It was a good two or three weeks before Hughie was persuaded to get up and see if he could do any better. 'Protest songs were all the rage in those days and so were talking blues — Peter Lyn Hayes' "Life Gets Tedious, Don'

'In my Liverpool home': on location at the Pier head, and folk night in Gregson's Well

Royal favourites: joking with Prince Charles after a Liverpool gala, and meeting the Queen after the Liverpool Empire Royal Variety Performance to mark the opening of the Kingsway tunnel

It" was a classic of its kind. I didn't think I had much to protest about — life was quite good, even then — but I had written a talking blues about dreaming of a win on the football pools. I'd called it "The Talking Football Pools" and so I sang that.'

He still does; in fact, it's become a Hughie classic, full of his dry humour ('Filled in the coupon using family birthdays and grannie's bust measurement, which always turned out to be Third Lanark . . .') and contorted rhymes ('The strings were made of solid platinum, with diamond pegs to tight an' slacken 'em . . .') It's been updated through the years (it no longer has references to Horace Bachelor and Charles Clore), and remains a firm favourite.

Hughie's sense of humour and distinctive voice made him an instant hit with the Samson and Barlow crowd, so that when Stan Francis left the group to concentrate on guitar making, Hughie was an obvious choice to take his place.

'I said fine, because by then I also knew an awful lot of songs. For a start I had the Burl Ives repertoire in my head, and quite a lot of other American stuff as well. Gradually it began to catch on. We aimed to get people interested in folk and went for audience participation from the start. We still believe that's important. Folk is more approachable than lots of other forms of music — it's do-it-yourself music, if you like. There seems to be no mystery about it.

'Yet once you really get into it and get the poetry of it, you get a different sort of mystery. Once you start reading the Child ballads and listening to all the different variations, you get into supernatural things and old folk customs and suchlike. A lot of people learn history through these old folk ballads, though it tends to be biased, depending on who wrote them or what part of the country they're from. That's especially true of Scottish ballads.'

Hughie met Chris, the girl he was to marry, in 1959 — in a taxi they shared from the Pier Head. He said he'd marry her if she learnt to play the banjo . . . 'Which I did, not because I necessarily wanted to marry him, but because it was a challenge,' she insists. 'Come to think of it, marriage to Hughie was a challenge too.'

They were married in 1963 and now live in a house overlooking the Mersey. (Hughie swears the river gets cleaner every year.) Once the home of a shipping family, their house even has a flagpole in the garden. 'We had the idea of running up all the flags of the shipping lines that have used the port on it — but then the sailors might get the wrong idea and think this was a refuge or something.'

She still has her banjo, which she bought from Stan Francis, but has not found much time to play it since she became a mother to their two children, Rachel and Daniel. But before the family came along, Chris helped to run the Wash-house Club in Liverpool, and sang with another city folk group, the Bothy Folk.

'I had sung Gilbert and Sullivan when I was younger, but had always been put off folk music by the way we had been forced to "enjoy" it at school,' she explains. Gradually she came to like it, and attended Spinners evenings at Samson and Barlow's, as well as performing herself.

She was the only one of the Spinners' wives to guess she might be marrying a professional musician. The last of the four to take the plunge, it was obvious to Hughie — who by that time had risen to be a departmental manager at the fancy goods factory where he worked on Liverpool's Speke trading estate — that soon the Spinners would have to make their minds up between a full-time or a minimal musical future.

Chris's swansong with the Bothy Folk was a riotous evening at Liverpool Empire with the Dubliners. 'What a way to go,' she remembers. 'Ronnie Drew, the one with the gravelly voice, was centre stage when the safety curtain came down on him.' Already anaesthetized with a fair amount of alcohol, he wasn't flattened but merely propelled across the stage, yelling, 'I'll have 'em for that . . . I'll have 'em!'

Chris put her banjo away after that spectacular night, and swears she didn't open its case for fully another ten years. When she did, she found a half-empty bottle of whisky tucked inside!

If Tony is the Buck's Fizz in the Spinners cocktail of success, Hughie is very much the dry Martini. Over the years his ability to sing unaccompanied ballads has developed, so that he has become one of the acknowledged masters of the art. He has, it must be said, also gained quite a reputation as a clown. 'The humour in our act started originally to shut Tony up. In the early days he would go into lengthy speeches extolling the virtues and beauty of folk music — all very laudable — but after a while, to lighten it a bit, we would start interrupting him with a few ad libs. It's always nice, anyway, to end any introduction to a song with a laugh, unless it is a sincere one, or a sad ballad or something, so that's where the wisecracks came from. And they had to be sharp one-liners to stop Tony in mid-flow!

'We don't script things or say "This is my new joke . . .". We tell it, and then it becomes a Spinners' joke. So at the end of one number while the lads are tuning up or selecting their instruments for the next, the person who's left at the mike talks to the audience and keeps them entertained. We never all turn our backs on the audience together. We need them with us all the way, so we don't think it's fair to leave them alone.'

Hughie's being from Liverpool helped as well. It's true what they say about Scousers — they really do seem to have the most highly-developed sense of humour, and Hughie is no exception.

His best remembered routine was to dress up as the Sugar Plum Fairy at the Spinners' Christmas concerts at the Phil and lead the audience in 'The Twelve Days of Christmas'.

'I said to the audience one year, in all innocence, not quite realizing what it would lead to: "I don't know about you but I can never remember what comes next, whether the geese-a-laying come before the maids-a-milking or whatever. So I've devised these signs you see — 'cos I've really learnt it this time — to help you remember too and cue you in."

'Well, the next thing I remember, the routine is getting developed and choreographed almost and telly producer Nick Hunter asked me if I fancied dressing up as a Sugar

Plum Fairy and doing it on the Christmas Show. So they made this creation for me in Barbara Cartland shocking pink, and a wand — I was insistent on a wand. It's the old tickling-stick syndrome, I guess — and there we were. It was launched.

'I did a Christmas tour, too, in this frock I remember — and people still come up and ask me to do it as though they only saw it last year on the box, whereas it must be about five or six years since I last did it. If something's good it's not a bad idea to leave it while it is good. Being fat and forty is not a good recommendation for leaping about in ballet skirts. Mind you, it might look even funnier now . . .'

They also spun

In the early days a striking part of the emerging Spinners sound was female — Tony's sister Joan and his wife Beryl, along with later addition Jacqui McDonald, were all Spinners at some time. It was when Jacqui left, initially to go solo, that the Spinners decided to remain as they were — an all-male group.

Joan was eighteen and still at school when she bought her first guitar — for £4, from Mick Groves. 'They showed me three chords and that was it — I was in,' she remembers. 'Tony was a great turfer-in at the deep end. He would shout to me which chords to play, and if I lost my way or found myself in the wrong key, I'd stay in the background and strum — quietly.'

It began to get interesting at the Cavern. Joan remembers Lonnie Donegan coming and complimenting her on her singing of 'When I'm Single'. She didn't altogether share the Gin Mill's love of skiffle, but endorsed their move towards folk when the scene began to go electric. 'At Samson and Barlow's we were a gang which became a group. I loved to sing the long unaccompanied ballads, while Tony and the others would pepper the programme with blues and funny songs as well as folk standards, to add that variety which kept it interesting.'

When Samson and Barlow's basement was full, the walls would run with condensation, and the Spinners would stand under the grating which let cooling air in from the street above — ideal until a bus rumbled past, usually during one of Joan's quiet numbers, it seemed!

'I was younger than any of the others, and needed looking after,' Joan confesses. 'Mick would walk me to the ferry or all the way home if I was extra late. A girl by herself and carrying a guitar case was a natural magnet for the yobbos — they'd yell, "Give us a tune then, girlie!" As a convent girl I couldn't always cope with this unwanted attention, so I'd get my glasses out and try to look intellectual. And on the bus, it was wise to stay downstairs and sit within sight of the conductor.'

Joan enjoyed being with the group, but found it increasingly embarrassing to find somewhere private to change. 'The boys were very gentlemanly about it all, but it was difficult having a girl around!'

Joan left when she went to university, with an open-ended invitation to come back when she'd completed her studies. 'But I knew I probably never would. Jacqui was so much better than me. It seemed natural just to fade into the background.' She still loves being on stage in front of an audience, and these days travels with her husband Bob Buckle to perform their own folk-based entertainment at theatres and clubs all over the country.

'I always wanted to be a singer, ever since I was a little girl. Carole Carr was my idol! But I was always conscious of my own limitations. I have shaky pitch control and under pressure I sing sharp. I can sing in tune when I'm relaxed.'

At university, and probably because of her involvement with the Spinners, Joan was a natural to take over the Folk Song Club. By then she had the contacts to invite guests, organize concerts. And later when husband Bob turned pro, as one half of a successful duo called The Leesiders, Joan did a lot of background work for them.

And what of the Spinners in those formative days? 'I think Mick saw himself as another Elvis at one time. He used to imitate all the actions — he wanted to be a star. Cliff, all credit to him, persevered and stuck at it. All the boys were helpful to each other. Tony cons me stupid — he still does — but he does carry you with him too. He's the eternal optimist.'

Jacqueline McDonald came from Yorkshire, from the

heart of Bronte country: her family kept a pub in Haworth. Her mother had been a music-hall artiste, but as a child Jacqui was more enthralled by the classics, and set her heart on learning the oboe.

'I well remember going with my mother on the bus to Harrogate to see what we could find. It was there we discovered that oboes cost something close to £70 — and I only had three guineas. So we said to the man in the music shop, "What can we buy for three guineas?" and came away with a second-hand guitar.'

Jacqui's success was probably helped by good timing, being in the right place at the right time. Always one to get involved, she went to Leeds to a Weavers concert on the only occasion they toured Great Britain (sadly, without Pete Seeger), and after the show found herself marshalling schoolchildren eager for autographs. The concert was an exciting one, including Sonny Terry and Brownie McGhee as well as Johnny Duncan and the Blue Grass Boys. Jacqui also met the promoter Roy Guest, who was later to introduce her to Tony Davis.

A few weeks later she left for Liverpool and teacher training college, only to find her move coincided with a Weavers concert at the Liverpool Empire. So she went along, went backstage again — and bumped into '6 foot 7 inches of loveliness, who turned out to be Tony'.

They got talking, and Tony invited her to Samson and Barlow's to hear the Spinners. 'The first Friday I turned up I sang two songs (one of which was a yodelling song, one of my favourites then), and — as Joan was about to leave — I was asked if I'd like to be a regular.'

During her time with the Spinners, Jacqui switched from guitar to mandolin, which better suited her style, and her clear voice and sunny disposition added a delightful aspect to the Spinners' appeal for her two-and-a-half-year stay with them till 1961.

'The Spinners were mostly married by then, and it seemed to me (wrongly, as it turned out) that with those sort of responsibilities there was no way they'd turn down safe careers and go professional,' she says. 'Also, it was a very lonely existence for a single girl on the road. The boys had their families to go back to, but I wanted to make more friends.'

If Jacqui thought the boys would not turn pro, it was her professional attitude to entertaining that Hughie reckons taught them a lot. 'She had a perkiness and a boldness in her approach to things — probably came from her mum,' he reckons. That professional touch turned the Spinners from a collection of singers into a group, but on one occasion Tony's 'show must go on' attitude hit Jacqui like a slap in the face.

'When my father died in 1960,' says Tony, 'it was after a long and painful fight against cancer. The Spinners had a concert to do the night after he died, and my mother advised me to go and do it. It would have been what he wanted, and there was nothing more I could do at home. So I went — but it shook a few of our friends and relatives. And it shook Jacqui too — I'm afraid she didn't speak to me for weeks.'

Occasionally a friend would accompany Jacqui on gigs to give her a bit of female company — there was Marnie who shared the driving with Cliff, and later Bridie O'Donnell, with whom Jacqui eventually formed the popular folk duo Jacqui and Bridie.

'I don't regret leaving the Spinners,' she says today. 'Every other week I seemed to have tonsilitis trying to make myself heard beside them. But I do regret not having the same success — who wouldn't?

During her time with the Spinners, it was Pete McGovern (who penned the enormously popular 'In My Liverpool Home') who suggested that Jacqui should take up the mandolin to complement her singing voice, and it is an instrument she has very much made her own.

When she teamed up with Bridie, they began their own folk club at the Coffee House in Wavertree, Liverpool, and it remains one of the city's favourite folk rendezvous. Over the years, Jacqui and Bridie have taken their own brand of entertainment to Germany to entertain British troops, as well as to America, and every year they spend time in Scotland where they have built up a substantial following.

Of those who have been victims of Tony's mania for

chucking people in at the deep end, perhaps not surprisingly the most willing, enthusiastic and most often picked-on has been his wife Beryl.

'I remember when we were first engaged, before he went to college, Tony said to me, "I've bought you a lovely present". He also said it was made of wood, so I thought, "Great. It'll be something useful for our home, like an ironing board or a clothes horse." In fact, it turned out to be a guitar. I thought "What in heaven's name do I want a guitar for?" '

Tony soon showed her — he taught Beryl a few chords and together they got a spot entertaining the customers in the Kinkaju coffee bar in Liverpool, Tony perching on a stool as he still does to compensate for his height, with Beryl playing softly in the background.

'I was just beginning to enjoy it when he went to college, and took my guitar with him — to teach himself to play. Then my brother brought me another guitar from Japan, and with those two instruments we started our skiffle group.'

There was a certain amount of parental opposition to Beryl's playing with the Gin Mill — even when, by then, she had two to protect her, husband Tony and new recruit Mick.

'Tony, Mick and I used to do the interval at Wavertree Town Hall. There always seemed to be a policeman about every five yards outside, and the lights were dimmed with newspaper shades — it was a real dump. And all the Teds would be there in their crepe-soled shoes and velvet collars, swinging their chains . . . Tony would hiss, "Don't look at them — just keep playing. You'll be all right." '

The Gin Mill played a lot of city clubs and venues before getting a regular spot at the Cavern, and it was outside the Cavern one night that Beryl fainted, being heavily pregnant with her first daughter Susan.

'They were so nice to us that night, that after she was born it seemed natural to take her to the club to show the kids. She had a knitted babygro on and was getting passed around the cellar . . . and when she came back to me she weighed considerably more and she jingled. They'd unzipped her babygro and stuffed coins inside! I must have found £3 or more in shillings and half-crowns down her jumper.'

Beryl stayed on when the Gin Mill became the Spinners and moved to Samson and Barlow's but, as the Davis family increased, she retreated more into the background, to help deal with the mounting number of fan letters and enquiries for the group, and with their publicity.

'I don't think either Joan or myself considered staying with the Spinners. And after the family came along I didn't hanker to go back to performing. But you could say we always played each ball as it came along.'

Some of their strokes were immense gambles too — or seemed so at the time. 'When we took the St George's Hall for the first time for a folk concert, we charged five bob any seat — and it worked. The place was full. Then Tony said we'd try for the Philharmonic, which was a completely different proposition. He took a whole month's housekeeping to put the Spinners on at the Phil (Merseyside's affectionate name for the Philharmonic Hall in Hope Street, home of the Royal Liverpool Philharmonic Orchestra). I was working it out: "How are we going to live? I'll buy lots of porridge oats, just in case . . ." I was really worried. But I needn't have been. In the event we got our money back and a bit more — and we did it again, and again.

'I remember going home and going to bed after that first Phil. It was our first big concert, and it had been recorded, and it was fantastic and the audience were marvellous. I thought, tomorrow morning it will be just like the films, with big headlines in the *Daily Post* and everybody cheering. I couldn't sleep all night. But it wasn't like that at all, of course. Next day everyone was carrying on as usual, and I thought, "Was that success?" It made me realize it's only the same as doing any job — you do it the best you can and then get on with the next thing.'

Although she had no particular hankering to perform again, Beryl has been known to get involved in recent years. 'Tony bought me an accordion, and I thought, "That's nice. I must learn to play it sometime." Then he got an invite to open the Bristol Boat Show, and he agreed, and said he'd bring John McCormick along to play bass, and Beryl would play accordion, so I thought I'd better get stuck in.'

Beryl sailed down to Bristol for the show on board the *Francis Drake*, in the teeth of a gale which gave the ketch quite a battering — while Tony and John went down by car.

After the Mayor had said his piece and Tony had declared the show open, and with the Royal Marines Band lined up along the quay with lots of children around, Tony said, 'Right, now we'll have a rousing chorus of "Blow the Man Down".'

'That was my cue,' says Beryl, 'to run through the crowd clutching my accordion and stand in front of that immaculate Royal Marines line-up in my oilskins and play. It wasn't very good, I must admit, because it was my first time; but I thought at least Tony would say: "Well done, darling, you were marvellous."

'Instead he turned to me and said, "You played it too slow!" '

If Jacqui and Joan were attracted to appearing on stage and being entertainers, Stan Francis was more like Beryl — happier being a backroom boy, and an occasional performer.

He was a Spinner for the first six months of their existence and later, during the 1960s, was a member of the Fishermen, another Liverpool folk-based outfit, whose driving force was Brian Jacques. But mostly Stan is renowned for his guitars, immaculate hand-made instruments, both six- and twelve-stringed. Hughie called Stan 'the Brunel of guitar makers' and his meticulous approach probably owed much to his grounding as a draughtsman and engineer.

He made a guitar for Lonnie Donegan after meeting him at the Cavern, and after Lonnie took a liking to Stan's own twelve-stringed instrument. But his biggest break came when he met Pete Seeger and Rambling Jack Elliott at

Liverpool's Neptune Theatre. Seeger was also impressed with Stan's twelve-string guitar, and ordered one for himself. He even said he might be able to get Stan some orders from the States. 'He went back to America and I thought no more of it — until I started getting these inquiries from New York, Los Angeles, Illinois. Apparently Pete had kept his word, and even wrote about me in an American folk magazine.' And so Stan found himself making guitars and shipping them out across the Atlantic. 'In those days (1961) it cost £15 to pack, ship and insure a guitar for the States,' he says.

Stan also made guitars for Tom Springfield ('I used to make them with triangular holes to the soundbox, and Tom is clearly holding the guitar I made him on the cover of one of the Springfield's LPs') and for Brian Jones of the Rolling Stones ('He sent his chauffeur to collect it in a Rolls').

Tom Springfield's guitar was also used by the Seekers, and when it was sent back to Stan for overhauling it was clear it had been well used. 'There was no major damage, like someone sitting on it or anything, but there were lots of scrapes and scratches that come with playing it a lot. That gave me a nice feeling, to know it had seen good service.'

Stan hasn't made a guitar since around the mid-1970s but he still gets requests to mend them. Nor does he miss performing — 'I used to do some guest spots in one or two folk clubs, but it got so that to be a successful folk entertainer you needed to be a raconteur as well as a singer. Some folk entertainers are really better comedians than they are singers or guitar players.'

Of the Spinners as guitarists, Stan says that Mick was probably the best guitar player at the start ('He was good at busking along with any song you cared to sing'). Hughie was different, more precise, while Cliff in time and with enthusiastic practice, could top them all in his own way.

He has guested with the Spinners, notably at their twenty-first anniversary concert at the Liverpool Philharmonic. 'As I get older I forget the songs, but if you sing them at longer intervals, people don't notice so much . . .'

Stan was the quiet man of the Spinners, immensely

likeable and talented, he has a great feeling for folk music. But he also likes taking life at his own speed, and found the weekly grind of having to perform and the necessity of learning new songs tiresome. He much preferred his own leisurely pace and the satisfaction which came (for him) from making things. 'You could say I just didn't like the discipline,' he explains. He also found some of the attitudes off-putting. 'Some people were obviously coming along because it was the trendy thing to do. They soon fell by the wayside, but for a while the scene was riddled with phonies. The same thing happened with the trad jazz revival. Those playing jazz on Merseyside now are those who do it because they enjoy it and because they want to.'

Sorting out the stayers was one thing, sorting out the purists from those with wider interests was another. 'It also seemed easy in the folk field to get over-dedicated to one aspect of it. There were some groups for whom "She Moves Through the Fair" would be a pop song. It can still be hard going. At some clubs you can hear nothing but Child ballads all night. Truthfully, it gets a bit dreary unless you're a devotee. Most people in my experience come to a folk club to be entertained.'

He still goes to the Spinners' club, but to listen not to perform. 'I don't always take my guitar with me. It smacks too much of "I've come to sing for you. Please ask me to play". There is no way you can "just happen to have" your guitar with you. You might "just happen" to have a mouth organ in your pocket, but a guitar is different. It's like those television chat shows where the interviewer says to the guest: "Are you going to give us a song?" and the orchestra "just happens" to have the right score for the right number right there.'

He is also full of admiration that the Spinners have kept their folk club going in Liverpool for so many years. 'They're unique in that respect — you can still see them in their original informal setting. It's like going to see the Beatles playing at the Cavern still . . . it just doesn't happen with other people. Imagine Jimmy Tarbuck still cracking jokes at Fazakerley Labour Club.'

Now we are four

From the early days the Spinners made a conscious effort to stay together as a group — a resolve that hardened after Jacqui left them to go solo. After the quick turnround in personnel in those early years between the Aigburth Conservative Fête and Jacqui quitting, everyone believed that would be the end of the Spinners.

'Even we found ourselves wondering how we were going to cope without a girl in the line-up,' admits Mick. 'But it turned out well. Whereas previously the quiet songs had been left to Jacqui, now Cliff or Hughie could do them. Previously we had either done the noisy, the dirty or the funny — now we had to do the lot. Our repertoire was completely reshaped.'

'When Jacqui left our immediate thought was to replace her,' says Hughie, 'to get the vocal balance right, and we thought anyway that a girl's voice was desirable to the sound we were trying to create. But I don't think any of us fancied holding auditions and all that again, so we set to and rehearsed and found we could do it on our own. We missed Jacqui, but four was a better number to take round. We could fit into the Austin Cambridge quite easily.'

They had all agreed that they would always sing as a group and not accept solo engagements — Cliff was asked to do Caribbean evenings on his own, Mick would be approached by what Tony jokingly calls 'the Catholic Mafia', Tony was asked to lecture — but initially they wouldn't do it. They had seen too many good groups and bands break up because of this, and their policy of strength through stability has paid off.

So has their cooperative approach to running the Spinners. Each had abilities and experience outside of showbusiness that made them ideal partners to share the work of keeping the group on the road. Cliff was able to drive and look after the transport arrangements, Hughie would look after the money, Mick would see to the sound and lighting while Tony, with his flair for publicity, would, with Beryl, do the bookings and make sure their name was known. This did not come from a personal mistrust of managers or agents. Initially when they started sharing the work, they were all still semi-pro and it seemed to make good sense. Equal shares of the spoils for an equal share in the burdens.

'There was a pioneering spirit about it,' says Tony. 'We all worked bloody hard. Cliff saved us literally hundreds of pounds nursing our vehicles from one gig to the next and spending time under the bonnet keeping the engine tuned. Mick is a good statistics man and keen on the technical side. He likes to keep lists of what songs we've sung, how long it takes us to get anywhere, the way we went last time — a great fund of information. Hughie had been an ace book-keeper and it seemed natural that we should all put our talents to use.'

When the group turned pro in 1964, they had £1,000 in the bank, their van (which was paid for) and a full date book from September till Christmas which would take them from the South Coast to the Scottish Highlands, and involve one nightmare journey in deep snow from London to Edinburgh in what were pre-motorway days. Not for the last time Cliff got them through. The van had been converted by craft teachers from Tony's school, and an upholsterer whom Hughie knew had kitted out the back with two padded bench seats which folded out into a comfy bed where they could curl up in their sleeping bags while Cliff drove through the night.

'It was all a question of control that made us start doing things for ourselves,' explains Mick. 'But even now when something goes wrong on stage, and I've told the lad operating the lights and sound what to do, it doesn't stop the others having a go at me — that's when it gets a bit discouraging. There are days when I think "Blow it — we'll pay someone, and he'll travel round with us, and he'll know exactly what needs doing; and I can relax before a concert knowing it'll be all right." But you can't rely on other people. They're not infallible either.

'We've always had top management, and been glad of it, but we've never needed a roadcrew — mainly because we haven't had to take round our own p.a. system, except in the very early days. Now, however, the whole scene is coming full circle, and so many groups are taking round their own sound systems that quite major concert halls aren't renewing their old equipment. It can be disconcerting when mikes die on you one by one in even the best halls — so maybe the day will come when we'll have to start taking our own again.'

'Through the years we've been on the road, we've seen a lot of people come and go, mostly through mismanagement, or others taking them for a ride,' says Cliff. 'So we decided quite early on that we wouldn't let this happen to us. We work as a unit — we need one good accountant, one good manager and booking agent, one good PR person, but the rest of the jobs we share among ourselves.

'That way we know the job's done right, the way we want it. It doesn't mean that we haven't had our rows over the years, but on the whole it's worked, and it's a system I could recommend to any group on the road; keep control of the thing yourselves. It's hard work but it's worth it in the end.'

If Cliff's musical ability had to be nursed, his love of cars was instinctive. He was taught to drive in an American Dodge ('a big black thing, like Al Capone used to drive . . .') by one of his mates in the electrical industry, and was soon transporting them between home and site, wherever they were working.

It was therefore natural when the Spinners took off that Cliff should be the group's driver and look after their transport — 'Though in those early days I had to be persuaded to drive through the Mersey Tunnel. I hated it. I

MISSIONARIES OF CHARITY

54A LOWER · CIRCULAR ROAD · CALCUTTA 16 · INDIA

17th February, 1977

The Spinners & Friends
C/o Co-Workers of Mother Teresa
29 Molyneux Close
Huyton, Liverpool, L36 6DL

Dear Spinners and Friends,

I know it has taken a very long time, but at long last, I am happy to give you the good news that we have been able to purchase an ambulance for our Raighar Branch for their work among the poor and sick. It is being used as a mobile dispensary cum leprosy clinic and the sisters are overjoyed that they can reach the poor more easily.

I am enclosing herewith two photographs of the new ambulance with the inscription "A Gift from The Spinners and Friends through War on Want."

This ambulance is made in India and we will be able to get spare parts when necessary without much difficulty.

Thanking you once again for your great generosity and self-sacrificing spirit which has made it possible for our Sisters in Raighar to have this beautiful ambulance.

God bless you
M. Teresa MC

Tom Sweeney, of the Co-Workers of Mother Teresa, at the wheel of one of the first ambulances the Spinners donated through War on Want to her work, and a letter of five years later, thanking them for another

All in a good cause: Cliff busking outside the Liverpool Playhouse, for the Variety Artists' Benevolent Fund, and Tony (with the stick he used before his hip replacement operation) and Mick chatting to passengers on a Mersey ferry while making a public information film for the National Blood Transfusion Service

think that's what gave me more confidence on the road than anything — having to drive through the Tunnel.'

Cliff enjoys his driving, though, and takes it seriously. 'When I'm at the wheel I concentrate. I don't like to talk — I just get on with the job. Every nut and bolt I used to know in all the cars we had, and if there was a squeak or a rattle that shouldn't be there I could hear it before the others and know something was wrong.'

His own taste in cars has veered towards BMW over the years, though his habit of buying in cash and on impulse has left salesmen nonplussed. 'I went into this Liverpool showroom and said to the guy, "I'll have that one, and can you have it ready by Thursday." He said, "Sure," but when I went back on Thursday it was still in the showroom. So I said to the manager, "Do you want to sell that car or not?" Turned out the salesman just hadn't believed me!'

After a brief flirtation with a 3-litre Capri which scared him rigid (and probably was the reason for his hair turning white — that and vandals taking a potshot at it with an air rifle on the motorway, the pellet embedding itself in the driver's door), Cliff turned to Saab. For group transport, however, the Spinners tried a succession of Volvos which Cliff found a dream to drive but uncomfortable to sit in. So it was back to Fords, and a mixture of Zodiacs and Granadas, until Johnny Mack joined them full-time. A purpose-built van to transport them and their instruments on tour seemed a sensible idea. It also meant they could sit round and discuss the programme, even practise if they wanted, without the restrictions of being in a car, which would involve talking or singing to the back of someone's head.

So for their 21st anniversary in 1979, the Spinners treated themselves to their very own customized 'folks-wagon', a Ford Transit Turbo-van in which the group could travel together in comfort. But still Cliff did the driving.

Beryl Davis wasn't trained for all the things she's found herself doing on behalf of the Spinners over the years. 'I just used my imagination — after all, I trained as a florist.'

In the early days when the Spinners were looking for bookings, Beryl and her helpers simply raided the phone book and sent off notes about the Spinners and their folk club to secretaries of all the social and working men's clubs they could find.

Tony did most of the negotiations with the BBC, dealing direct with the contract department ('and screwing our fees up a bit each time') while Beryl did the donkey work. Her most consistent helper over the years has been Eunice Williamson. It's been a hectic partnership in which Eunice has done most of the sums. Trained in an accountant's office, she once told Beryl, 'If you need any help don't be afraid to ask.' Since then she's found herself addressing and posting thousands of *Spin* magazines, leaflets, posters, and working out a budget for Beryl's ancillary interests, like music publishing, for the Spinners also produce regular song books.

'Eunice can visualize numbers the same way I can visualize music,' Beryl explains. 'I value people who do their share of the work. She takes a lot off my shoulders, and I'm grateful.'

The Spinners naturally have always benefited from good management, first from Lyn Dutton and latterly from Colin Hogg, while Beryl and Eunice look after all the odds and ends that crop up. In the beginning they approached one of Britain's leading PR men, Leslie Perrin, to do some promotion work for them. 'He was extremely useful, and opened a lot of doors for us. We were lucky that people seemed willing to put themselves out for us. And still we have lots of contacts we can turn to for advice — and you don't always expect that in showbusiness.'

Tony also pays tribute to Les. 'When we had our Tamla Motown mix-up over the Detroit Spinners, it didn't cost us a penny. Les Perrin was a saint, and he taught Beryl all she knows. Lyn Dutton, too, was the manager we wanted, a manager who fitted our image, not pushy or showbizzy. We were concert artists rather than razzmatazz and Lyn was ideal. We could work well with him, and built the foundations of a successful career. He left in the end because of his heart condition, but he continued to do the concert bookings with Colin taking over the management. Eventually Colin took over the lot.'

'The Spinners were told early on that they'd never be a big success,' remembers Beryl. 'They'd never be stars because they were too approachable. It was thought you had to have a mystique, stand back from your audience. You couldn't let little old ladies come up to you in the street and greet you like their long-lost sons. But the boys would say they sang to communicate, to contact people. If someone wrote to them after seeing one of their shows and said, "I was feeling terribly low and depressed, but you've made me happy again," or "I hadn't touched the piano for twenty years, but after going to your concert, I went home and started playing again. You've got me singing round the house once more," they knew they'd got through. That's what the Spinners sing for — not for others to put them on a pedestal and say, "Aren't they great." But to communicate.'

Sowing and growing

Determined to continue their research into the roots and traditions of folk music, in the late 1950s the Spinners were making regular weekend trips to London, to play at the Troubadour Club — the capital's premier folk venue at that time — and also to raid the library at Cecil Sharp House, home of the English Folk Dance and Song Society.

The usual drill in the days before they turned pro was to rush from their day jobs, pile into their old Bedford van and, with Cliff at the wheel, head off down towards the capital on a Friday evening.

This was also in the days before motorways so it was a long and tiring journey, at the end of which they were required to do a late, late spot at the Troubadour before crashing out in sleeping bags on some understanding soul's spare-room floor. Sympathetic friends who took pity on them in those pioneering days included Sydney Carter who had a small flat in a large house in the Gray's Inn Road, and Eric Winter, who used to reserve his couches for the Spinners at his North London home.

Saturdays were then spent browsing through the shelves of the library at Cecil Sharp House, and Saturday evenings singing in the Society's Folk Cellar, followed by another late, late Troubadour session. And as if that wasn't enough excitement for one weekend, they might even take in the Folklanders' Club at Potters Bar on the way home.

The Spinners' own club at Samson and Barlow's in Liverpool, one of the first regional folk clubs in the vanguard of the English revival, was also a cellar, and that seemed appropriate. 'Folk music was very much an underground scene in those days,' explains Hughie. 'We would go to London and play in some incredibly weird places, and often play through the night too. At the Troubadour it was an established custom to bring down the early editions of the Sunday papers about four in the morning, and we'd still be playing.'

The boys got £3 between them playing the EFDSS Folk Cellar, but shared £10 at the Troubadour, not to be sneezed at in those pre-decimal, pre-inflation days.

Those weekend trips to London were really one mad rush — Hughie sometimes leaped into the van still wearing his white storeman's coat. It was he who kept them solvent in those days by doing the books, working out what they could afford. 'It was just a list of outgoings and incomings — more of the first than the second! We weren't making anything out of it, but we seemed to manage to cover our petrol and food.'

But things were beginning to happen for them. Their reputation was growing, they began to make their first LP, *Quayside Songs Old and New*, at Cecil Sharp House, and Samson and Barlow's was beginning to bulge at the seams with interested folkies — so many that they had to move upstairs to a larger room.

And still they continued with their daytime jobs, and their weekend trips to London. 'We had great nights at the Troubadour,' remembers Mick. 'It was one of those London spots where whoever was in town would drop in — Bob Dylan, Tom Paxton, Paul Simon and Pete Seeger.'

Martin Carthy was a regular at this Old Brompton Road venue, and on occasion — along with others — he would play through the night, just for the hell of it. 'The standard of the floor singing was good, and you always got solid guests. It was a smashing place.'

As the folk revival spread, other clubs opened with other guests for them to meet. Hughie remembers a time at the Marquee Club when a chap came up to him and said, 'I've written this amazing song.' Hughie listened and said, 'You must be mad — who's going to buy that?' The answer was millions, for the song was 'I Love My Dog' and it made the songwriter's name. He was Cat Stevens.

In the early 1960s, as well as rummaging through the rich and varied treasures of Cecil Sharp House, and soaking up the accumulated enthusiasm and enjoyment of the folk scene, the Spinners met Cheshire fruit farmer, folk singer and song writer Leslie Howarth, one of those whom Tony calls a 'seminal influence' on their development. It was at an English Folk Song and Dance Society festival in Manchester. 'Leslie was a fruit farmer from Kelsall,' recalls Tony, 'devoted to folk songs and ballads, Manchester United and Lancashire Cricket Club. He had a venerable white beard and taught me so much about singing and life and burgundy wine. At that time Beryl and I had two very small children, not much money and no motor car, and every year when the strawberries came, he used to have us all over to his farm for a weekend. I remember our daughter Susan at the age of three tottering through the strawberry beds, falling flat on her face, and shoving fruit into her mouth, just lying there.'

Leslie was the man who wrote 'Here's to Cheshire,' and these idyllic summer weekends would often coincide with the visit in later years to the Spinners' club of guests like Jeannie Robertson, the great Scottish ballad singer, or Hedy West from the Appalachian Mountains.

When Leslie died at the age of sixty-nine his sons held a wake for him, with the Lofthouse Sword Dancers from Yorkshire, a local ceilidh band and the Spinners. The whole event was recorded and Leslie sang his own epitaph on the recording. 'Yes,' says Tony, 'we learnt a lot from Leslie about a whole host of things.'

Because of their involvement with the English Folk Dance and Song Society, in 1960/61 Tony and Mick were able to persuade the local authority to back them in establishing what was the country's first Folk Song Workshop in Liverpool.

'It was great, because it taught us as much as it taught the students. We always had to keep one step ahead of them by reading more books and listening to more records. So for two years we battered our heads into what was going on in America and here,' says Mick.

The clincher for many of their students was the free guitar lesson that was thrown in each week — not necessarily the comparison seminars on the Child ballad in England and America. Magazines coming out of America taught them a lot about the transatlantic scene and its developments, and they studied the notes of Cecil Sharp and other English collectors. 'It was a lot of fun and hard work — and very valuable to us,' adds Mick.

Out of the Folksong Workshop came a song based on Eddie Cochrane's 'Summertime Blues', called 'Woodchoppin' Blues', adapted by Don Howarth with heavy Liverpool overtones. The lyric described how kids would raid propsies (Scouse for old houses, preferably empty) for wood for the bombie (Guy Fawkes' bonfire).

At that time the BBC in Manchester were doing a documentary on street life and were looking for urban songs to describe certain situations. Mick told them about 'Woodchoppin' Blues' and they liked the idea.

'I conned the headmaster,' says Mick, 'into letting the kids out for a morning to take part. I sold it to him on the basis of it being an educational experience for them — which it was. So the BBC filmed them roaming over this oller (waste ground), and provided them with wood, old doors and ceiling joists, plus the axes to break it up, all to the tune of this "Woodchoppin' Blues". I got nowt out of it except a morning off school like the rest of them, but it was good fun.'

By now the Spinners were beginning to take off — they had already gone up in the world, progressing from Samson and Barlow's basement to a larger upstairs room to accommodate their growing faithful band of followers.

Now they were also learning things like presentation, harmony and performance. Jacqui had knowledge of harmony and an instinctive feel for arrangement — with her, the boys became a group, and began to add polish to their enthusiasm. It was no surprise that their reputation as well as their repertoire grew.

But were they reaching the right audience? Tony remembers the late red-bearded Dave Henry, who took the money on the door in the early club days, once saying: 'While we're sitting here in our folk club, singing folk songs, the folk are somewhere else, doing something completely different.'

At that time it was probably true, for 'folk' was still a cult thing. But the Spinners' aim was to fulfil Cecil Sharp's dream and give folk songs back to the ordinary people, making them part of the mainstream of people's enjoyment again. 'And whatever our critics may say, I reckon we've done it,' adds Tony. 'Thousands come to hear the Spinners, and maybe hundreds go on to listen to other aspects of folk music. If, of those, dozens become devotees, then we've done our job.'

'We were always alternative music,' says Mick. 'But eventually we were booked not just because we were alternative music, but because people were becoming more aware of folk, and accepting it as part of the entertainment scene. We always used the word "alternative" in the best sense of giving people a choice — they have the telly, or the radio, or their video, or they can go to a disco, or the cinema or theatre, or to a club — like a folk club. The choice is quite large these days — it makes me cross when people say it isn't, because it is and it always has been.'

When the Spinners started going out of the clubs on to a wider circuit they found themselves doing a May Ball in Cambridge one year, with the John Mayall Blues Train.

'We got shown to this room to change, and the guy said he'd bring us some food and drink. But after a while I got fed up with waiting so I said to the others I'm going in search of a drink,' says Cliff. 'I went down to where the main action was and everyone was in penguin suits and the girls were in ball gowns and I was in my working clothes if you like. Anyway, I managed to catch the eye of the man behind the bar and asked for a drink. He said, "Certainly sir," and handed me a glass and a bottle of champagne!

'I shot back upstairs to the others and said, "Look , man. Look what I got. I ask for a drink and he gave me a bottle! I couldn't believe it." '

As the rooms they played in got too small to accommodate the increasing number of eager folk who wanted to hear their music, the Spinners sought out yet another city venue at Gregson's Well public house, moving there in 1963. 'I still think the best years in our club life were at Gregson's,' Mick says, but after twelve years there they would find themselves forced to move. And the Triton, where they now play, has undoubtedly retained that friendly, good-humoured atmosphere in which they thrive.

But, back in the early 1960s, while pondering on how to reach an even larger audience with their brand of folk entertainment, Tony and Beryl took time off to visit Liverpool's Royal Court Theatre and enjoy the delights of Michael Flanders and Donald Swann, then travelling in *At the Drop of Another Hat*, their hugely successful and entertaining revue.

They were flabbergasted to be mentioned from the stage by Flanders: this was acknowledgement of how their fame was beginning to spread, and how impressed others had become with the Spinners' enthusiasm for their music and their dedication to spreading its enjoyment. Flanders and Swann had actually got the audience to join in a rollicking chorus of 'Mud, Glorious Mud', at the end of which Michael Flanders had wheeled himself to the edge of the stage, glared in that mock-serious style of his, reminiscent of James Robertson Justice at his wickedest, and said: 'Very good, but if you stick together and practise, maybe one day you might just be as good as the Spinners.'

'We were an island unto ourselves, really,' explained Donald Swann. 'There weren't any other artists at that time doing precisely what we were doing, and we didn't have any close friends in showbusiness, but the Spinners were among those we were getting to know. And we shared their approach to audiences — we wanted the audience to be involved, and to be on our side.'

Flanders and Swann were in fact following in what was an essentially English tradition of two fellows around a piano singing reflections on life, with a topical acid flavour. The Western Brothers had done similar things for years on radio, but Michael Flanders went further, taking folk tunes and reworking the words in a light-hearted revue parody, with a degree of sophistication which won him and Donald many friends on both sides of the Atlantic.

Flanders and Swann were together almost as long as the Spinners have been. 'Theirs is a great witness, and I'm jealous of it in some ways,' admits Donald Swann, 'though Michael and I were together for as long as we were allowed to be together.' (Flanders, a wheelchair-bound sufferer from polio and a champion for the disabled, died in April 1976.)

So, meeting Flanders and Swann at Liverpool's Stork Hotel, after the Royal Court show, Tony and Beryl invited them to Gregson's Well. As the steps to the upper folk-room proved an insurmountable obstacle for Michael's wheelchair, Donald came alone, and was impressed.

'Have you ever thought of trying a theatre, old boy?' he asked Tony. Tony said they had, but that they had not been able at that time to convince others that the Spinners might be able to fill a concert hall.

'Prove them wrong — book yourselves,' he was told. 'After all, that's what Michael and I did. You never know what you can do until you try.'

So with hearts in mouths, empty wallets and fingers tightly crossed, Tony and Beryl booked Liverpool's impressive St George's Hall, not sure if it was a wise or foolish venture, whether many would come or just a few. It turned out to be a huge success, and spurred them on to book the Liverpool Philharmonic Hall that Christmas. So began one of Liverpool's enduring and most enjoyable traditions — Folk at the Phil.

As the group became increasingly professional, they decided to wear a stage uniform — initially simple pale blue shirts and ties, with toning trousers. Hughie also grew and wore a droopy Viva Zapata moustache for a time. 'I don't know why I did it,' he recalls, 'except to prove that I could. It didn't suit me at all. I shaved it off the night before we first played the Albert Hall.'

Reaching out

It is a moot point whether the Spinners were in fact the first folk group, and one of those things that doesn't matter all that much anyway. It is a matter of pride and record, however, that they have survived longer than any of the other groups which sprang up in the early days of the Folk Revival.

At that time there was a marvellous group called The Thamesiders, with Red Sullivan and Long John Baldry, as well as the Clarion Singers with Ian Campbell, Luke Kelly and Dave Swarbrick among their number. Steve Benbow had his Folk Four and Roy Guest his Wanderers, when the Spinners began their trips to London.

But these 'groups' all had changing personnel and interacting personnel. Harry Boardman, for instance, would draw a group around him for a concert, while artists like Shirley Collins, Dominic Behan and Stan Kelly, calling themselves Folk Song Unlimited, would get together for a concert.

They were freewheeling days of joy and discovery. The Spinners' club was among the first to open outside of London, alongside the Topic in Bradford, Harry Boardman's club in Manchester, and the Folk Song and Ballads Club in Newcastle, home for many years of the High Level Ranters.

Through their music and their club the Spinners have never claimed more for themselves than that they sought to interest people in the British folk song tradition, to give them a flavour of the rich treasury that was their heritage, and to point them in the direction of more disciplined and diverse performers if they wished to explore folk's colourful tapestry along a different strand. They have done this by taking folk music to a wider audience, not only through their concert tours, but through radio, through television, through folk festivals, and through the English Folk Dance and Song Society.

The Spinners have never put themselves forward as the great saviours of English folk music, yet they have done much to ensure that its traditions have thrived and been nurtured by succeeding waves of enthusiasts.

They are especially grateful to the Society, not only to Cecil Sharp House, but to those faithful local members who gave them their first introduction to folk songs round the green baize table all those years ago.

The Society has played a vital part in their folk education, and they in turn have remained loyal, with an affection like that which successful scholars have for a favourite tutor.

S. A. 'Nibs' Matthews, director of the English Folk Dance and Song Society, is generous in his praise of the Spinners. 'We have a high regard for them,' he says. 'There is no denying they have pointed a lot of people towards folk music over the years, they have opened up the whole folk music scene.'

Both Tony and Mick have served terms on the EFDSS executive.

'The Spinners have done a lot for the Society and people in the Society admire them for their contribution and their entertainment, and their loyalty. For people who have made it to the top they are still very nice people to know.'

'Our motives were threefold,' Tony explains. 'To learn as much as we could about folk music, to pass it on to our club members and to a wider audience if possible and — above all — to get people to sing.'

This meant breaking through that traditional English reserve. It was all right for factory girls to sing along to

'Music While You Work' — that seemed natural enough, as did singing in church. But in a concert hall, with people you didn't know ... 'We still get told today: "You'll never get this lot to sing." But anybody will sing if you create the right atmosphere and show them you really want them to.'

Hughie says the Spinners were the first group in Britain to do this — to go out with the express intention of involving people in the folk revival and from the start it was a labour of love. In fact, the Spinners insisted they wouldn't turn pro — almost right up till the day they did so.

'I meant it, quite genuinely. I thought turning pro we would lose something,' says Tony. 'I really enjoyed my teaching too — but then Pete Seeger asked me: "How many kids can you reach in a year?" If you go out singing like we do, and like the Weavers do, you can reach thousands . . . That realization clinched it for me.'

For Tony, as for many other English singers in the revival, Pete Seeger was what he calls 'a seminal influence' — 'Not necessarily what he did with the Weavers, but what he did on his own, and his own approach to folk music. That influenced me greatly in those days.'

Having turned professional, however, the Spinners were so buoyed up by their own emotions and their own involvement that they expected instant conversion of the masses to folk music.

It didn't happen quite like that... and so then they learnt about presentation and style and form, and started to put together the package of humour, playing and singing they have evolved and presented successfully all these years.

Several big breaks happened during 1963/64 before the Spinners finally decided in the autumn to turn professional. Philips released their first LP on the Fontana label (called simply *The Spinners*) and this coincided with their first St George's Hall concert, which sold out three weeks beforehand, without any advance publicity.

Philips launched the Fontana label before a collection of record dealers at the Blackpool Audio and Hi-Fi Fair, and it was journalist Eric Winter, then folk columnist of the

Melody Maker, who persuaded them to include the Spinners as part of the presentation. The dealers were absolutely knocked out by their spontaneous display, and the Spinners, who had initially only been asked to do one morning presentation, found themselves asked back for a swift repeat that afternoon.

Hughie and Chris had got married just before that Blackpool Fair, and were conveniently on honeymoon in nearby Lytham.

On the morning the Spinners were due to appear at the Fair, Hughie took his bride of a few days on a trip into the resort, where he 'just happened' to meet the rest of the boys, 'just happened' to have his guitar with him, and they 'just happened' to be performing... Chris learnt early that this was something she'd have to live with!

So word got back to Jack Baverstock at Philips in London, who was told, 'You must go to Liverpool and hear the Spinners — we must have them on Fontana.' Baverstock was indeed due to go to Liverpool to hear a number of emerging beat groups; and there the Spinners found him, visibly bored and battered after hearing solid rock'n'roll for the best part of the day.

So they soothed him with a couple of well-chosen folk lyrics, at the end of which he brightened and said, 'Boys, I'm in a position to offer you a contract.' Hughie, with immaculate timing, pulled a bottle of whisky out from his tunic, and replied: 'Splendid. I'm in a position to offer you a glass of Scotch!'

But it was Hughie who almost missed the group's first recording session. Fontana had fixed it for a Friday evening in London, bearing in mind the four lads' working commitments; and the Spinners had decided to take a British Eagle flight from Speke airport and hang the expense. With time ticking away to take-off, Hughie was nowhere to be seen. Eventually a van roared up from the nearby industrial estate and out leapt Hughie, still in his white factory overalls, not having told his employer he was knocking off. A quick change, the waiving of a few departure rules, and they were away at last.

Following the success of the St George's Hall concert,

the Philharmonic Hall was booked for the first time in April 1964 and Fontana recorded the whole show, eventually releasing that on two LPs, *Folk at the Phil* and *More Folk at the Phil*, the first of which was released to coincide with their turning professional, and with their first television series of 'Dance and Skylark'.

It was a heady way for any group to start their career in showbiz proper.

If the name 'The Spinners' seemed logical in retrospect, it gave them much trouble initially — and still does from time to time.

The group subscribe at not inconsiderable expense to a press cutting agency, and have been known regularly to receive, not only their own cuttings, but those of other groups called Spinners . . . and the annual reports of the Company and Guild of Cotton Spinners.

In 1958 the film *Alive and Kicking* was released, starring Sybil Thorndike, Kathleen Harrison and Stanley Holloway as elderly participants in a 'Good Life' cooperative on a remote island in the Irish Sea. The theme song, which bore the same title as the film, was released as a single by the Geoff Love Singers, backed with 'Green Grow the Rushes-O', and for some inexplicable reason they called themselves the Spinners for that one release.

'This record kept bugging us for years,' says Tony. 'It probably just beat us to the punch by months so, originally to get round the confusion, we called ourselves the Liverpool Spinners for one EP, then thought "This is ridiculous. Why bother?" and went back to being plain Spinners again.'

Still their troubles were not over. It seemed a popular and obvious choice of name for other groups in the folk revival, and the Spinners found themselves on the verge of legal action several times. All their potential namesake rivals bowed out gracefully — until Tamla Motown came to town.

In the United States, the Spinners meant four lads from Detroit who were blowing up a storm in the charts and grabbing fans in the UK too. But when their records starting appearing over here and a concert tour was arranged, things got pretty heavy.

Tony again: 'Our PR man, Leslie Perrin, told the Tamla agent nicely, "You can't call them the Spinners over here. The confusion will be tremendous." Sadly, Tamla took the stance: "Who are these other guys anyway? Just some two-bit folk group." Leslie said: "They're well respected, have a huge audience, have done regular tv and radio series, concert tours . . ." Tamla retorted: "Yeah, well our guys have topped the charts. Forget it — we're coming in." '

So the Spinners had trouble on their hands. A High Court injunction was slapped on the Tamla group restraining them from using the name, a battery of top people in the music business were willing to back the Spinners in their cause, and in the end Tamla had to concede.

The Tamla group became the Detroit Spinners in this country while the Spinners added Liverpool to their name for American releases.

But it rankled for a while — the American record company tried an album calling its group the Motown Spinners and that was stopped. Concert bills were produced with 'The Spinners' in capitals and 'Detroit' in smaller lettering and they were withdrawn.

Worse was the reaction of sections of the music press, in tune with Motown but not necessarily on the folk wavelength. 'It was all a bit childish,' Tony adds, 'and the saddest part of it was we never met the Detroit Spinners, though as far as we can judge they're four nice guys who haven't had a bad word to say about us either. But the confusion was bad for a while. We had people writing to us from the States saying, "We went along to a Spinners concert and were disappointed not to see you. There were four black guys up there singing soul." Maybe one day we'll get a chance to put that right.'

In the early days of the folk revival the Spinners communicated their love of folk music not only through their club, their concerts and their recordings, but also through *Spin* magazine.

'There was a competition at the club — I thought it was a daft idea to start with,' admits Beryl. 'I wondered who was going to type up all these magazines anyway — and who was going to buy them.' She soon found out.

The first issue in October 1961 was a great success, so much so that people began writing in to place subscriptions. Unfortunately all those who had helped to bring out the first magazine in a blaze of enthusiasm found that it had all been such an effort that they melted into the background, leaving Beryl with a demand, but not much to fill it with.

'To get it off my back (which I never did) a few other people helped me bring out a second issue — in fact we brought out several before putting it on a proper footing. The Spinners lent me £10 to start it off, and in time we produced six issues of *Spin* a year, circulating five thousand copies each edition, and it ran for ten years. It was never more than a kitchen table effort, but it was a very good kitchen table effort.'

Copies went to universities and libraries all over the world — to the Vatican, behind the Iron Curtain and to the university in Jerusalem, as well as to the Library of Congress in Washington and Johannesburg public library. ('They kept re-ordering a certain back number,' Beryl remembers. 'It must have gone missing about twelve times. It was the one with the words of "We Shall Overcome" inside.')

Leslie Howarth was a regular contributor, penning a column called 'Well Met'. He also wrote about ballads, while Stan Hugill wrote about the sea and shanties in his 'Bosun's Locker' column. Even the late A. L. Lloyd, the much-respected folk chronicler and performer, was an occasional contributor. 'We paid our writers a guinea. It was all we could afford, but at least it showed we appreciated their efforts and didn't take them for granted.'

Spin served the need of a growing audience to fill in some of the background to the folk revolution, delve into its history and air a few controversies. It was never a folk newspaper, with a list of who's playing where. 'We tried to keep it interesting,' says Beryl. 'It taught us as much as it taught our readers. We used to find it fascinating.'

Reflecting the growing interest in folk, the English Folk Dance and Song Society were soon involved in organizing folk festivals, and the first was held at Keele University in 1962.

'Rory McEwan brought together everyone he could think of,' remembers Tony. 'It was full of missionary zeal — like an English Newport.' Paul Oliver, Stan Hugill, the blind Rev. Gary Davis, plus Hedy West, Bill Clifton and a host of sundry spiritual and gospel singers from the States joined Ewan MacColl and Peggy Seeger, A. L. Lloyd, Fred Jordan and Jeannie Robertson . . . 'It was a great coming together where you could rub shoulders with traditional singers and television stars and get involved in a session with the greatest. But there was no "them and us" about it,' adds Tony. Eventually the festival moved to Loughborough and became a successful annual event.

In addition to the established folk festivals, there was also the occasion when — partly to obliterate sad, bad memories of riotous behaviour at his previous jazz festival as well as to restore his faith in human nature — Lord Montagu opened the grounds of Palace House, Beaulieu, to the folk fraternity in 1966. But instead of riots, those who turned up had a more traditional English hazard to contend with — rain. 'It was,' remembers Mick, 'the world's first underwater folk festival.'

The Spinners were there alongside Tom Paxton, Julie Felix and more — and it poured. Diz Disley was compèring and though he could see a mass of brave souls huddled under capes, tarpaulins and golf umbrellas, many more were sheltering under the trees, the bushes, the stage, even in the loos where they appropriately sang sea shanties.

'I tell you what,' Disley said, 'We'll auction the fishing rights to the press box,' — which was now clearly awash. Indeed the local county paper, the *Hampshire Chronicle*, published a picture of the sodden scene and headlined its report 'The Soggy, Soggy Few'.

In the midst of all this the Dubliners arrived. They came down by train from London and were well lubricated after the journey. Backstage, all they wanted was a drink. Mick showed them the small paper cups they were all using and Barney said, 'Don't want one like that. I want a real drink. How about a bottle?'

So the Spinners ordered up for them — vodka for Ciaran, brandy for Luke, and went to the bar to explain. 'The bottles behind the bar had optics on them,' said Mick, 'so we kidded the young barman "Well that one's only got about, say, five shots left in and at two shillings a shot, that's . . ." and so on through the line, till we got him mightily confused and snaffled the bottles off the bar for a fraction the price they should have been.

'Well, the Dubliners couldn't have been friendlier — and they also couldn't understand how we'd been there so long and were still sober while they were well away. The reason was simple — we'd driven down and we hadn't had that much to drink once we got there. But it didn't do our reputation any good. The Dubliners were convinced the Spinners were hard drinkers who could hold their liquor and for years afterwards, whenever anyone said to them that they were drinking too much, they used to say, "If you think we're bad, you should see the Spinners!" It wasn't true — but then we paced ourselves. They were always hell raisers.'

In Liverpool, which was becoming one of the prime provincial centres in the folk revival, local broadcaster, writer and musician Fritz Spiegl organized Scouse Nights at the Bluecoat Chambers, with not only the Spinners and Jacqui and Bridie, but also Frank Shaw telling his Liverpool tales, Glyn Hughes in his dapper suit strumming his rhythm guitar ('The Tommy Steele of the local folk scene,' remembers Bridie), plus Stan Kelly, who wrote the evocative 'Liverpool Lullaby'. In the interval the audience was treated to authentic Scouse delicacies, including tasty 'wet nellies' — stale bread peppered with raisins and soaked in cold tea.

Then, in 1969, Tony and Beryl organized a day-long Folk Festival in St George's Hall where, as well as local singers, they invited folk dance and song expert Ethel Anderson from Cecil Sharp House to run a folk workshop and Johnny Handle from the Ballad and Blues club in Newcastle to give advice on music making.

Bass meant

The Spinners used a number of bass players to augment their cheerful sound, and by the 1970s had settled on two regulars — Bill Brown, who did southern concerts with them, and John McCormick, who did the north. There had been other bass players before these: Harry Archer and Bob Duffy, while Spike Heatley was a favourite for recording sessions.

They met Bill Brown in Salford through radio producer Peter Pilbeam. Bill had been at the College of Music in Manchester and worked with the NDO. Pilbeam called him in to back a number of groups for a radio folk series he was producing, and Bill hit it off with the Spinners straight away. Hughie says of Bill Brown: 'He was tremendous. It was the first time I'd heard a proper musician play bass.'

When he moved to London, Bill found himself increasingly called on by the Spinners to accompany them at concerts in the Queen Elizabeth Hall, the Fairfield Hall, Croydon, the Royal Festival Hall . . . and further afield. As his workload increased, he suggested they try John McCormick for northern concerts. 'They were understandably reticent at first, but when they eventually got round to calling on him, they rang me up and said, "Hey. He's marvellous!" And I said "I know. I've been telling you that for the last six months!"'

In the mid 1970s Bill reached a stage where he had to choose between his other commitments and the Spinners. 'It was impossible for me to do more for them. It would have been unfair to them to have me hanging on.'

So Bill left, as he fancied the variety which other work could offer. 'And, besides, it was getting to be a sensible move for them to have a regular bass player.'

But he has many happy memories of Spinners concerts, recording sessions, television and radio shows over the years. 'The biggest surprise was the first Christmas concert at the Phil in which Hughie dressed up as a fairy . . . They hadn't told me about that. In all the run-throughs it had been glossed over, and then on stage during the concert he suddenly appeared in all this finery. I must admit I nearly dropped the bass and rolled on the floor with laughter. It was the funniest thing I'd ever seen them do.'

Bill has nothing but admiration for the Spinners' professional attitude to their work. 'They are the Rolls-Royce of folk groups,' he says. 'I've never seen them stuck for words. As soon as they get on stage, they're perfect, professional to a "t".'

'Count' John McCormick was another product of the jazz and skiffle scene on Merseyside. He even played with Lonnie Donegan's band at the Cavern, and can remember becoming involved in some memorable late-night jam sessions. But whereas the Spinners chose the folk road, Johnny stayed with the rock scene until National Service called him away. 'Apart from a brief spell with English Electric I've always made my living as a musician,' he explains, and he played in various clubs on Merseyside and Manchester. 'With two friends I used to make up a nightclub "Play it again, Sam" trio, playing nice cabaret jazz. There was work around if you got to know people. Being bold and hardfaced, we survived.'

For about three years in the 1960s he worked in a Manchester club called the Whisky-a-Go-Go, and during that time the boss decided a female singer would complement their line-up. 'So we auditioned about twenty singers and ended up with a very good young girl, who had just left the Eric Delaney band through homesickness after touring American bases in Europe. Her name was Elkie Brooks.' The quality of the cabaret at the Whisky-a-Go-Go was good and word soon reached Granada TV. Their top talent spotter, Johnny Hamp, would drop in from time to time, and began booking them on a regular basis.

Then 'Count' John got a real break. Ray Ellington heard him play and offered him a job with his quartet. 'He was very big at the time — it was soon after the Goon Shows had finished — and I mulled it over for about six weeks before accepting.' There was a chance of getting established in London, but there was also a gamble of being out of work for long periods as Ellington paid no retainer. Johnny found there was a certain amount of radio and television work, but an equally large amount of hanging around. In the end, he opted to leave the Ellington set-up and try something he had sampled once before — the regularity of playing on Union Castle cruise liners plying between Southampton and Cape Town.

When that finished, the natural thing seemed to be to return to Manchester, where he had more contacts than in London, and pick up the threads once more.

It was then he met up with the Spinners again. He had known Bill Brown for some years — they were old mates — and when Bill decided to cut down on his Spinners' commitments, he recommended John to the group. He did his first gig with the Spinners in 1971 and joined them as full-time bass player and musical arranger three years later. The fans now look on him as the fifth Spinner — and the one question he gets asked 'till it hurts is: 'When are you going to wear the Spinners' uniform? Instead of standing in the background like a permanent first reserve, when are you going to don a first-team shirt?'

'It gets as wearing as the old question every bass player gets asked: "How do you get it under your chin?" I think too it gets embarrassing, or annoying, for the lads when fans keep pestering, asking when they are going to make me a member of the group. People don't realize, don't understand, that they've been together since 1958, and all the arrangements they've made over the years have been made on the basis that they *are* a quartet. It would involve a massive administrative shake-up for me to become part of that. I suppose it would be easy for them to say, "Put this shirt on to keep the fans happy, to keep them quiet," but really I don't expect it. I've only been with them a relatively short period of time. Much of what they are has been built up over the years without me. Truly, the whole business worries the fans more than it worries me.'

Being a part of the group, and yet apart, does have its hazards. He often finds himself refereeing the inevitable behind-the-scenes altercations, smoothing the flare-ups which are part of the life of any touring group. 'But when they want me to take sides, when one of them says, "At least you agree with me, don't you, John?" then I bury my head in my newspaper and pretend not to hear. You have to know when to stay quiet.'

On musical matters, however, he's not so neutral. 'I get on my high horse now and again, and try to instill a fresh approach into some of their material. It's hard to unlock an old arrangement that they've been doing for years and get them to do it a different way. But new material demands a new approach, and on anything to do with music, I can make my stand. That's what they pay me for, after all.'

The danger with any job you've being doing for any length of time is getting into a rut, and the temptation for artists who've been around a long time is to coast through a concert tour. 'I remember being on stage with Gene Pitney,' John says. 'He'd come over to this country, where he hasn't had a hit for many years, and do the old songs in a particular order... then maybe come back in eighteen months time, and do the same thing all over again. There comes a time when you feel you don't need to try any more. That's the big danger.'

The Spinners, he reckons, keep themselves sharp by joking on stage. There's never time to switch to auto-pilot and go through the motions. There's always someone feeding a line that requires a response.

How different is playing bass for a folk group from playing jazz and the other kinds of music John had known? 'You have consciously to try not to play too many harmonic changes. The Spinners don't like "busy" bass players. I had to listen, and not assume that they would play the changes I was used to. A certain amount of trial and error was involved. Originally, I would struggle on stage with a bass music stand and a mound of sheet music. That was too much like hard work — it was much easier to make time and learn their numbers by heart.'

Not a natural singer (not many bass players are!) John had a rare solo on their 1981 album *Around the World and Back Again*. More usually he is to be found playing a variety of instruments on their records and radio shows. 'I even played concertina on an Anglian TV show at the time of the 1978 Tall Ships Race. I sellotaped off the notes I didn't need and got by . . . but it was nerve-racking stuff.'

John sees his role as taking the weight off the group's shoulders so far as musical arrangements are concerned, and he much prefers radio to television. 'Television people are naturally picture-conscious, but I often get the impression that the sound comes a poor second to the picture. Whereas on radio they pay attention to the right balanced sound.'

The Spinners' West African tour in the autumn of 1977, sponsored by the British Council, was marred by illness for Johnny McCormick. He now lightly calls it 'sheer bad luck' but, at the time, it must have been touch and go. He was taken ill on the plane between Cameroon and Ghana, with what appeared to be a simple case of malaria. 'It seems they assume it's the twenty-four-hour variety unless it doesn't clear up in that time, in which case it's the forty-eight-hour variety unless it doesn't clear up in that time, in which case it's something more serious,' he explains.

It was something more serious — it was, in fact, typhic pneumonia. 'I've always felt that if I hadn't had the jabs before I went I wouldn't be here now,' Johnny adds cheerfully.

Replacement bass player Kenny Baldock was flown out to complete the tour, and Johnny was nursed for a fortnight by Ghanaian medics, for whom he has nothing but praise. He was allowed home at the end of the fortnight only because Liverpool has a famed School of Tropical Medicine where his recovery could be monitored.

Johnny now likes to sail to relax and thoroughly enjoyed both the Tall Ships Race of 1978 and the Spinners' involvement with the Ocean Youth Club. 'It's not so easy for me, however, as I feel I owe my wife and daughter as much of my time as I can when I'm not travelling. So usually I unwind by playing my bass!'

He is a welcome dropper-in at a number of jazz haunts on Merseyside — the Philharmonic pub, the Hunt's Cross Hotel, the Bradford. 'After a couple of days of unwinding and doing nothing, it's good to go out and play a spot of jazz. I can feel drained after a few hours but it stretches the fingers — and it stretches me too. I enjoy it.'

Like the others, John had no idea things would go on this long — but he's extremely grateful they have. As for the future? 'I'm not really sure, though an orchestral job would be nice. The Phil would be ideal . . .'

But for the moment he's happy to stick with the Spinners for as long as the public want them to stick together. 'We get longish and regular breaks which is good, for it means I can plan other things. And then when we get together again it's like a fresh start. Of course, the run up to Christmas is the killer. There's usually a full commitment of concerts, a lot of travelling, then just when you're feeling knackered, there's a television special to do, and the Liverpool Phil Christmas do, where you feel you want to give of your best. Everybody's really strung out by the end of all that. But providing we get past Christmas Eve without any lynchings we know we're all right for another year.'

Colour or creed

The Spinners have always left those around them in no doubt as to what they believe in, and although not called upon to suffer for their ideals as publicly or as punishingly as their American counterparts, they have nevertheless had their worrying moments. But their stand for racial harmony seems to have been accepted from the start and to have been an asset in winning them friends, rather than losing them any.

Cliff counts himself lucky not to have been the target of much racial abuse over the years with the Spinners. Certainly his colour has never mattered either to Spinners fans or to the group. Perhaps his early acceptance of England as his home, as well as an early acceptance by those around him of Cliff as a self-contained person rather than a figurehead for black causes, has helped. Politics is something that bothers him not at all — he has led a quiet uncontroversial life outside of the group and has certainly done nothing to antagonize either his adopted white friends or his black brothers.

One or two confrontations still stick in the mind, however. One occurred when the Spinners, on the way home from a concert, stopped at a roadside bowling alley near Birmingham. While Cliff parked the van, the rest of the group went in. When he came to go through the door it was made clear to him, by the proprietor, that he wasn't welcome. Tony, sensing something was wrong, went back to Cliff's aid — and when the owner saw this giant of a man advancing on him (and perhaps he recognized him and Cliff by then) he quickly changed his mind — Cliff could come in and join the rest.

But the damage had been done — the Spinners left, and didn't go back.

Cliff has never gone seeking confrontation and incidents like that usually sadden and embarrass him rather than move him to anger. There was another time, however, outside the Kraal Coffee Bar in New Brighton when two or three drunken youths were abusing Cliff and he was advised by the rest of the lads to seek refuge in the group's car.

Tony again leapt to his aid, and remonstrated with the drunks, who then started kicking the car. 'I suppose they thought if they couldn't take it out on Cliff they'd take it out on the vehicle,' says Tony. 'But they couldn't have chosen a worse course of action. Cliff was out of that car like a shot, brandishing the starting handle, and they fled! It was all right to call him names, but touch his precious vehicle and they were in real trouble!'

In any case, Cliff is usually the one to defuse likely confrontations with his pleasant sense of humour — or just an unconscious outburst.

'I thought Tony would have splattered that guy in Birmingham against the wall, but me — I would have let it go. The number of times I've come off stage after a hectic concert and said "Man, I've been working like a black tonight," and people laugh. I don't mean to say it — it's just an expression that comes naturally.

'There was another time when we were entertaining the marchers on the 1981 Liverpool to London Right to Work March and we'd gone down to Wolverhampton to see them. It was the night of the FA Cup final replay, and after our concert we watched it on television. Spurs were playing Manchester City and City were leading. I'm not particularly a fan of City, but I did want to see the Cup come north instead of south, so I was willing them to win. Then Garth Crooks scored the equalizer for Spurs and before I knew what I was doing I was on my feet shouting,

"Oh, you black idiot!" and everybody around me collapsed with laughter.

'I also like watching cricket, and when the West Indians come over I usually support England. That makes people think a bit too. They generally look at me a bit strange, as if to say: "Whose side are you on, anyway?"'

Jacqui McDonald remembers a time when she was touring with the Spinners and went to wake Cliff one morning. He was sleeping in the group's Dormobile, and when she rapped on the window, the curtains parted and Cliff's bleary-eyed gaze met hers — but his face was covered in white grease which he'd smeared on for a skin complaint. She was initially taken aback, and then burst out laughing. Cliff quickly caught on, grinned back, and said: 'Well, darling — if you can't beat 'em, you gotta join 'em!'

Cliff's wife Janet has her own direct way of defusing trouble. 'Very occasionally we'd find some drunk would make a few uncomplimentary remarks. I'd just give them as good as they gave, and they'd shut up. I'd let them know in no uncertain terms they couldn't speak about my man like that.'

Cliff, she explains, has never had a chip on his shoulder, and they have brought up their family to take all the jokes and the jibes — and not let it worry them.

Cliff sums it up: 'I have been very lucky — I know that — I have not had any bad treatment from people in this country, to bother me or my family. And as a group the Spinners have not had to preach non-segregation. We just have to get up on stage and demonstrate it. And we sing our songs about Black and White, "together we learn", and people get the message without us having to hammer it home. Just being on stage and living what we sing is enough.'

Contact between the races has therefore been a natural Spinners' theme over the years, and 1979 saw them in Liverpool Cathedral for a Multi-Racial Week concert which also included Indian dancers, a Chinese dragon dance and a West Indian steel band.

Another colour problem hit the Spinners after a few

years, following the success of 'The Orange and the Green'. Unlike 'Black and White', which was a lyrical plea for racial harmony, 'The Orange and the Green' started life as a knockabout fun song about the difficulties experienced in one Irish family when their Catholic son falls in love with a Protestant lass.

The Spinners themselves are split — two Catholics and two Protestants, and the song, written by Tony Murphy, aims gentle barbs at the bigots on both sides of the religious divide. But they don't sing it now. 'As things got worse, we stopped,' explained Tony. 'It became increasingly difficult to get up on stage and have fun with this song, and then come off and find there'd been another bomb outrage somewhere and so many people were dead. The joke just stopped being funny.

'When I'm up on stage I don't consciously think, "I'm doing this for God,"' says Tony. 'Any religious feeling you have is within you, something you try to live your daily life by. So I wouldn't consciously offend anybody.'

Hughie adds: 'The religious side of folk music is something we've never gone out to cultivate deliberately, but inevitably it happens because it's there . . . not only in Sydney Carter's "Lord of the Dance", but in the traditional songs of the triumphs and struggles of ordinary men. It's something which can touch you deeply — you feel it.'

Cliff says: 'When we're on stage, or in front of the cameras, when we're actually working for other people, we have to remember it's them who pay us our wages, and we owe it to them to give of our best. So we'll try to carry on what we're doing now, and do it perhaps a little better every time.'

In considering the Spinners' relationship to 'politics', it is instructive to glance across the Atlantic for a moment. An American group the Spinners greatly admired was Pete Seeger's the Weavers, who suffered considerably because of the principled stands they adopted on various issues. Blacklisted during the McCarthy era, they nevertheless took their music from the picket line to the hit parade. It was said, and justly, that they cared more for their ideals than they did for commercial success — and yet success came their way because audiences and record-buyers recognized their genuine commitment and responded to it, finding more in their music than just entertainment.

(Age has a way of covering even the most rebellious with respectability, and when the Weavers got together for what was to be their final re-union concert in the early 1980s — the death soon afterwards of one of their number, Lee Hays, meant that there could be no more — Pete Seeger was interviewed on BBC's 'Newsnight' programme. 'Man, I'm so respectable now, something ought to be done about it,' said Seeger; but he still battles strongly for the things he believes in.)

In the early days of the British folk revival, before *Spin* magazine was produced, the folk song magazine was *Sing*, a mixture of topical left-wing opinion and traditional songs. Because folk songs were loosely labelled 'songs of the people' its adherents were labelled (and sometimes tended to be) 'lefties'. It's probably true to say that when the message in *Sing* became too overtly political, *Spin* found a market among those who wanted to learn about folk for folk's sake. Devon songwriter Cyril Tawney paid it the compliment of describing it as a running encyclopaedia of folk.

Since they were folk singers and got themselves involved in the early days in rallies for CND and the like, the Spinners also found themselves labelled as 'lefties'. In the late 1950s they were at the Liverpool University Students' Union giving a concert in the small Gilmore Hall, while next door in the larger Stanley Hall the then Lord Mayor and a hand-picked party of establishment figures were enjoying a theatrical evening. On their way out, being escorted by the Student Union President, the Mayor's party heard the music coming from next door, and someone said: 'That's nice. Who's playing?'

The party were told it was the Spinners and were asked if they'd like to go in. 'Not to hear that bunch of lefties,' and out they swept. They had just sat through a performance of Brecht's *Mother Courage* by the East Berlin University

Theatrical Ensemble. 'It was a ludicrous situation,' Tony remembers. 'We were told about it afterwards, and we reckoned it was only because we'd been given publicity the week before for taking part in a nuclear disarmament demonstration outside the American consulate.'

So how political are the Spinners? 'Depends what you mean by political,' Tony hedges. 'I don't consider nuclear weapons or apartheid to be *political* issues. They are *humanitarian* issues. I don't believe that anyone in politics should have anything to do with creating a world with nuclear weapons in it. It appals me to find politicians on all sides saying we must have nuclear weapons. Equally it encourages me to find politicians from all parties similarly committed to *not* having nuclear weapons.

'It's sheer logical common sense, not "politics", to oppose nuclear weapons.'

Over the years the Spinners have marched in support of nuclear disarmament, and against apartheid, and in 1981 entertained walkers on the Jobless March from Liverpool to London.

'We didn't see that as necessarily a political issue either — it was made political by default, because it wasn't supported by members of all political parties — yet it could have been,' says Tony. 'And when Tony Benn came along, the media immediately started labelling it "extremist". He went to a church service during the march, and when he came out the vultures of the press shoved microphones in his face demanding to know how he has the audacity to worship. He says, "I've been going to church since I was a boy. I've always gone to church." He was very good humoured about it in the circumstances. I think he's a great man, a marvellous man.'

But such a confrontation highlights an old dilemma. 'They used to argue how could people possibly build Chartres Cathedral or Notre Dame with people living in poverty in their shadow. Or, more recently, how could they build Liverpool Cathedral on the edge of Toxteth. But then, it's true — man does not live by bread alone. Spiritual welfare is equally as important as bodily comfort.

'We became dismayed by what appeared to be quite a

blatant and determined attempt to politicize any song you cared to name in the folk spectrum,' adds Tony, citing the late A. L. Lloyd's insistence that the old song 'The Demon Lover' must be from the manor house and not a song of the peasants, for the lyrics referred to the Devil as having a cloven hoof. The peasants, so the Lloyd argument went, were less fanciful, more realistic, and to them the Devil would be just a man dressed up in a goatskin. He would therefore have feet like anyone else. And then there was the song of the 'Cutty Wren', which Tony describes as 'a straightforward New Year song of revival and reincarnation'. Lloyd would insist it was a song of the Peasants' Revolt, recalling the days when the wren was a symbol of the people's uprising, and was carried on a pole at the head of the rebels. Despite these differences of interpretation, Lloyd still wrote guest articles for *Spin*, along with Pete Seeger, Fritz Spiegl, Alex Campbell and Paul Oliver. 'It was Beryl's baby, but in the end inflation broke her heart. She wound it up rather than keep asking subscribers and advertisers for more money.'

It is hard to believe that the Spinners and the other folk groups were considered 'new wave' or 'alternative music', but it's true. Certainly, the Spinners were instrumental in taking traditional songs off the library shelves, dusting them down and giving them back to the people. 'And when ordinary people got hold of folk songs again, and rediscovered this rich heritage,' says Hughie, 'the politicians who had been manipulating the scene for a while tended to loose their grip. For what the man in the street mainly wanted to use them for was what they had always been used for — entertainment.'

But a lot of the songs reflected hard times, and a lot of the industrial ballads tended to have a 'left-wing' message, being full of 'them and us' confrontation. That was what at first made folk music so appealing to Topic Records, for Topic was a branch of the Workers' Music Association. But Topic was also ready to record traditional singers, the old 'field' singers with memories full of traditional songs they had learnt when they were children and been singing all their lives.

'We were the first group to bring this music to a mass audience,' says Hughie. 'As well as going along to clubs and concerts and singing our songs, we would point people in the direction of Topic and the other labels recording these marvellous traditional singers, and try to encourage them to listen to the music and the singers we listened to.'

These singers could be found anywhere — in cities like Liverpool they tended to be pub entertainers whose party piece would be an old music hall number, in the country the chap in the corner of the snug, singing for his pint, would recall the rural songs of his childhood, passed on through gentle generations.

The Spinners did have one brush with the Communists, which shook them rigid and taught them a valuable lesson.

'We were told by the organizers that the visit of Harry Pollitt, Lancashire-born chairman of the British Communist party, was to a private meeting of Communist party workers, and we were being asked to provide the cabaret,' says Mick. 'And we were getting paid. Tony and I were still worried about it and went to our priests for guidance. Both of them said the same thing, more or less — if it's a private do and you're getting paid, just look on it that it's fewer leaflets they can print. If they think the labourers are worthy of their hire, being good Socialists you should take the money and run!

'Having therefore said we'd do it, we then found our name splashed all over Liverpool on posters advertising Pollitt's visit — we were horrified. After the concert, which we had committed ourselves to do, the organizer thanked us and said, "We must do this again." We left him in no doubt, saying in no uncertain terms, that we wanted nothing to do with any repeat performance. I remember him thumping the table and blazing: "If the Spinners think they can get anywhere in this country without our backing they've got another think coming!"'

Harry Pollitt wasn't amused either when Mick asked him about the ditty current at that time: 'Harry Pollitt is a Bolshie'. Mick had heard it sung in school playgrounds on Merseyside, and had seen it printed, even in Communist Party magazines, in praise of Pollitt. But Pollitt himself claimed it had been written by reactionary students to discredit him.

'Ours used to be a fairly firm group political commitment,' adds Mick, 'but it's more loosely left-wing now.' They were, however, quick to support the fledgling workers' co-operative at Kirkby Manufacturing and Engineering (KME), helping to raise money for a dream which for four short years brought jobs and hope to one of Merseyside's many depressed corners.

KME was launched as a workers' cooperative in 1975, after a number of firms, including Fisher Bendix, had tried to make a go of the works and failed. It had the backing of the then Minister for Industry, Tony Benn, and local MP Sir Harold Wilson. After swallowing £5.7m in loans and grants, it finally collapsed in 1979. Another enterprise the Spinners supported was the doomed Dunlop factory at Speke. Less successful even than KME, it too closed in 1979.

The Spinners also raised money for the Lofthouse Colliery disaster fund, with a night of mining songs, and then in November 1976 were invited by Ulster peace campaigners Mairead Corrigan and Betty Williams to sing at a Trafalgar Square rally, the climax of the Ulster Peace People's first mass march through London. Joan Baez also sang, and the platform contained the then Archbishop of Canterbury, Dr Donald Coggan, Lord Longford, and Lady Jane Ewart-Biggs, widow of Britain's ambassador to Dublin, who had been killed by the Provisional IRA.

'The Spinners have always been involved in what the Liberals would call "community politics",' says Mick. 'But we've always been a good mix — although Tony and I are Catholics we reflect different shades of the Catholic spectrum — and our strength over the years has been in our diversity, in retaining our individuality.' That strength has been emphasized over the years in their billing — concerts on stage, television or radio will invariably bill the Spinners by name individually. Most other groups are known simply by the name of the group — very few bill their members as individuals.

'It's just evolved that way,' says Mick. 'People have

recognized from the beginning that we are not just the Spinners, but four very different guys who have a part to play in the whole.'

Unlike Cliff or Hughie, Mick is politically active and is a member of Upton Labour Party on the Wirral, where he lives. Together with Tony and John McCormick he has joined a fairly new 'Arts for Labour' group, formed by performers, writers and technicians, dedicated to electing a Labour government, and pledged to advising any future Arts Minister on policy.

The group did a lot of singing and playing for CND and anti-apartheid rallies which weren't necessarily politically backed. 'It did worry me at the beginning, however,' confesses Mick, 'that there was strong Communist backing for the folk revival and the Communist presence was in evidence at a lot of these rallies. As a Catholic teacher I began to get a bit worried about all this. But then I met an old lady from the Quakers on a CND march and she told me: "Don't let it worry you. If you're pushing a wagon up a hill, and somebody wants to help you, you don't worry about the colour of their skin or ask them what their politics are. If you think it's worthwhile getting that wagon to the top of the hill, let them help. But don't let them put more on the cart than they'll push!"'

The Spinners have lent their names to a number of socially-aware campaigns, from mass X-ray tuberculosis scans in the 1960s (for which they wrote 'TB or not TB') to blood transfusion and fostering. They spearheaded a fostering campaign in the 1970s, by recording the Anne Swithinbank song 'Castles in the Air'. It won a national competition to find a song related to fostering and became a huge success.

Folk singers do generally tend to have leftish sympathies — and this meant that there was a paradox in the membership of the English Folk Dance and Song Society — most of whom tended to be professional people, right of centre, trying desperately hard to get inside a working-class tradition.

'I try not to lose my commitment to things I believe in,' says Tony. 'It's very easy to get flabby, morally flabby, as you get older . . . to say we'll leave the struggle to the young ones, we've done our share. We're constantly being urged to get involved with nice safe causes like the World Wildlife Fund. Nothing wrong with that, I'm all for saving the whale — but let's get our priorities right. It's a bloody sight more important to get involved with the World Human Life Fund. When you talk of endangered species . . . what about the starving children we've seen in West Africa, or the boat people, or the folk in India dying of famine with their homes being swept away? We *must* get our priorities right.'

Since about 1970, and through the Co-Workers of Mother Teresa, the Spinners have supported War on Want. Local organizer Tom Sweeney reckons that in over twelve years some £40,000 has been donated towards medical aid for the Third World, in the shape of ambulances and mobile clinics, and money for their maintenance and supplies.

Four are now in use by the Sisters of Mother Teresa in Bangladesh, India and Tanzania. Money raised by the Spinners and given by grateful fans has also gone towards relief work in El Salvador and the Lebanon.

One of the bonuses of this work and of being a Spinner, is the opportunity it gives for travel abroad. 'One of my most exciting tours was the one we made to Israel in 1975,' says Cliff. 'I was visiting places I'd only read about in the Bible, and didn't think I'd ever be able to see for myself. I'm not a deeply religious person, but I do have faith, and that tour was one of my greatest experiences.'

Africa, which they visited in 1977, also left a great impression on him and on the others. The poverty of the countries they passed through, and the way people lived, was in stark contrast to their own affluence and even to what we call 'poverty' in this country.

'That really got to us and we knew we had to do something. So we worked all the harder for War on Want,' says Cliff. 'What we do may be a drop in the ocean, but it's still a drop, and it's better than doing nothing.'

'All showbiz people get asked to do things for charity,' Mick adds, 'and a long time ago Lyn Dutton (then our manager) told us, "You've all got big hearts and I know you'd do anything for any deserving cause if asked. But you've also got wives and families at home and you have to earn a living." So he taught us to pick one specific charity to concentrate on.

'We thought about it a great deal and eventually chose War on Want, who support Mother Teresa. Any charity do we attend now we ask for a donation to War on Want as well, and all the money we raise goes to help Mother Teresa and the Sisters of Mercy, which is deeply satisfying to me as a Catholic.'

Of the four, Cliff was the one probably closest to poverty during his childhood in Jamaica — 'But it always seemed you could get food if you wanted it, for Jamaica is such a fertile island. But in Africa these people had nothing and no prospects of anything either.'

He and the rest are scathing about British attitudes to poverty in the Third World. 'Man, we live in palaces compared to them. Even our poor are rich compared to them.'

Africa did have its lighter moments too. While they were in Nigeria, the Spinners were on location up country for a television programme, when Tony noticed a group of small dark men watching him with great interest.

He later found out they were from a tribe of shepherds, who specialized in playing a primitive form of flute. So Tony offered them one of his whistles, and one of the men was eventually persuaded to play it. 'It was quite brilliant,' Tony remembers, 'unlike anything I'd heard before.'

Then, later, at Lagos airport, waiting for the plane home, Tony noticed that one of the heavily-armed sentries on duty was obviously from the same tribe. So he offered him a whistle too and, instead of tucking it away to play later, the sentry began excitedly to play there and then. The haunting music floated around the airport lounge, and even the sentry's commanding officer strolled by, nodding and smiling encouragement.

'I often like to wonder what would have happened if, say, a Gordon Highlander had been on sentry duty at Heathrow and been offered a set of bagpipes by a group of wandering musicians. I bet the reaction of his CO would have been slightly different . . .' Tony adds.

Royals and idols

An essential part of the Spinners' appeal is their informality of approach, and they've proved this works with anyone — including royalty.

During 1977 they were among the stars providing cabaret at Wakefield Theatre Club for a charity gala attended by Princess Margaret, president of the English Folk Song and Dance Society. They wanted to dedicate a number 'to the Pres', but rather than sing her the obvious 'Maggie May' they did four-part harmony on 'Twanky Dillo' and dedicated that to her instead. After the show, they handed her a copy of their record; and she told them that she had 'Caught your reference to the Pres!'

'Do you get to Cecil Sharp House often?' she then asked Tony, who found himself replying — before he could stop himself — 'More often than you do.'

By this time, both Tony and Mick had done terms on the national executive of the Society, and knew that Princess Margaret was a less than frequent visitor to its functions and committee meetings. It was also known that she had been turned off in the past — and it must be admitted, not without some justification — by a certain 'fuddy-duddy' air prevailing in the higher ranks of the Society.

Tony seized his chance to prove to Princess Margaret that things had indeed changed over the years. 'If we organized a ceilidh, would you come?' he asked. 'Will you be there?' she asked in return, expressing a preference not for the usual demonstration evening but for — in Tony's words — an 'informal knees-up'.

And that's what she got. Young members of the London Folk came along and danced with her, and the Spinners came and brought other fine singers to entertain her — and it was an enjoyable eye-opener all round. Tony adds: 'It was a very private affair, an internal informal night "for the Pres". We expected her to drop in for an hour during the evening, but in fact she came early and stayed until the end.'

British royalty still has some way to go to catch up with Scandinavian royalty for informality. The Spinners discovered this at the end of the Tall Ships Race from Great Yarmouth to Oslo, when they performed before King Olav and his family in a show that included Burl Ives, Liv Ullman, Sven-Bertil Taube, as well as Peter Gilmore and Howard Lang of 'The Onedin Line'.

Tony again: 'We were mixing with the guests after the show, and found ourselves chatting to a young woman who had a nasty-looking plaster around her foot. Cliff asked how she'd been injured, and she said someone with stiletto heels had backed into her at a garden party and broken her foot. I knew she was with the royal party but I didn't know for certain who she was. Then she asked if she could have one of our records. I said, "Of course. But how can I get it to you?"

"Oh just come up to the palace," she said, "knock on the door, and ask for Princess Astrid."'

The British tend not to treat their Royal Family quite so informally, but Prince Charles in particular has gained himself a reputation as man who enjoys a joke.

He was certainly a hit with Cliff when he attended a Liverpool Gala in the late 1970s. When Cliff met the Prince, he was still holding the outsize kazoo which he uses in the act to do Louis Armstrong impressions, among other things, particularly during 'Coney Island Washboard Roundalay'. The Prince said to him: 'If you'll excuse a well-known phrase or saying — I've never seen one as big as that before!'

Cliff said: 'I told him what I tell most people when they ask how it grew to that size. I left it out in the rain one night, and by morning, this is what I found! And we both had a good laugh about it. I could see Charles in the Royal Box during the show obviously enjoying what we were doing. That made me feel good. He asked me how my kazoo made that marvellous sound and I told him it worked on the old "comb and paper" principle.'

The Spinners count it a pleasure to be asked to perform for royalty, but Cliff perhaps even more than the others — and he likes things to be right on important occasions.

When the Queen came to Liverpool in June 1971 to open the Kingsway road tunnel under the Mersey, she was entertained at a special Royal Show in the Liverpool Empire.

For family reasons Tony and Beryl were late arriving at the theatre, and only managed to dash down the red carpet to take their places seconds before the Queen stepped out of her car. 'As we scuttled past the boys, I glimpsed Cliff out of the corner of my eye,' says Tony. 'He was giving me one of his looks, which said: "You've let us down again, Davis!"'

It was, and still is, a big thrill for the Spinners to meet their idols, the singers who influenced and entertained them so richly when they started out.

On one occasion, Cisco Huston, Woody Guthrie's famed collaborator on several memorable albums, came to Liverpool when Hughie was ill, and upset that he wouldn't meet Cisco, whom he'd admired for many years.

So after the Cavern set, everyone adjourned to Cliff's home where, specially for Hughie, Cisco sang a song into a tape recorder. 'Seeing as how Mohammed can't come to the mountain, I'll just have to come to you, Hughie,' he crooned.

'Hughie was delighted — really made up with it,' remembers Cliff. 'He thought it was a marvellous gesture. But then he lent the tape to Tony, and I don't think he's ever quite forgiven him for losing it.'

Mick also remembers a Bradford concert about that time, where Ramblin' Jack Elliott and Long John Baldry were appearing. Elliott launched into 'Tom Joad', Woody Guthrie's marathon ballad based on *The Grapes of Wrath,* which had most people in the club spellbound, except for a couple of boozed-up, spaced-out customers near the front. Their own private conversation was getting louder and more persistent until eventually Elliott stopped singing and silence fell.

Realizing they were now the centre of attention, the talkative two looked up to find Elliott staring into their eyes. 'Best damned song that ever was wrote,' said Ramblin' Jack and picked up again where he'd left off.

'It was beautiful the way he did it,' Mick recalls. 'What a way to shut people up.'

English audiences have a habit (as do American) of applauding solos in the middle of a number, or coming in too early with applause before the end of a song. Mick, Tony and Beryl went to hear the Gerry Mulligan Quartet at the Liverpool Phil one time, when Joe Benjamin did a solo during which you could have heard a pin drop. At the end there was a slight lull and some of the audience burst out clapping. Gerry Mulligan stepped forward, put his finger to his lips and said, 'You'll break the continuity.'

'That, too, was beautiful,' says Mick. 'I know the idea behind the applause — the audience only wants to please the artist, but just sometimes it can screw you up as well.'

Hughie's great idol was and remains Burl Ives. 'I first met him at the Liverpool Empire — he came around Festival of Britain time, and I remember being very impressed because his guitar had such a shine on it that every so often the spotlight would catch it and it would hit you in the eye . . . I thought one day, I'll have a guitar that does that.'

It was many years later that Hughie and the rest of the Spinners met up with Burl again — in 1978, at the time of the Tall Ships Race from Great Yarmouth to Oslo — and he was struck by the change in him. 'Of course he was much older, but offstage he struck me as a sad figure, like a worn-out machine. Mind you, he was over seventy — yet when he went on stage the old magic was still there.'

It was a genuine thrill for all the Spinners to play with Burl Ives at concerts in Manchester and Liverpool that winter. 'I was knocked out by that simple guitar style. It hadn't changed over all those years. Perhaps if he was a wizzo guitar player it would detract from the words — and he has got an incredibly pleasant voice.'

Hughie kept all his Burl Ives records, all the old 78s, and still plays them. Burl Ives to him and to many is a genuine folk hero.

If Mick considered himself the worst washboard player of the skiffle era, the most surprising exponent must be Deryck Guyler. The talented Wallasey-born comedy actor also has a life-long affinity with traditional jazz, which made him a natural to guest with the Spinners on several television and radio shows and on record, notably in 'Coney Island Washboard Roundalay'. They even teamed up with Sir Harry Secombe on second washboard to hilarious effect on 'Secombe with Music' for Yorkshire TV in 1982.

Guyler is fondly remembered for his Frisby Dyke character in Tommy Handley's wartime ITMA radio series (Frisby Dyke was an old-fashioned and highly-respected Liverpool store, and Handley, another Liverpool exile, christened Deryck with its name quite suddenly on the air). Deryck has always had a fond association with the city. His family in fact ran a jewellery store in Liverpool for over a hundred and thirty years until 1980. And the Spinners were more than happy to pay tribute to Deryck's friendship on 'This is Your Life', as they had to another old friend, Michael Flanders, in times past.

Sound on, vision on

Hogmanay to herald the 1960s, and at a Spinners' party held in Liverpool, Robin Hall and Jimmy McGregor lead the celebrations. Both had already begun their successful association with the BBC's topical 'Tonight' programme, hosted by Cliff Michelmore and with a vintage set of roving reporters including Fyfe Robertson and Alan Whicker. Folk was reflecting the mood of the times, and Robin and Jimmy's contribution fitted the programme format ideally, and they were to become pioneers in spreading the evangel of folk through television.

'We enjoyed coming to the Spinners' club,' says Jimmy. 'It was one of the better folk clubs around at that time, and they were one of the first to encourage the audience to join in, and be a part of the entertainment. I'm amazed but also glad that not only have the Spinners survived so long, but their club is still going.' Although they no longer sing together as a duo, Robin and Jimmy went back to the Spinners' current Liverpool home in the Triton for the twenty-first anniversary as well as appearing together on television in 1981 to celebrate the twenty-fifth anniversary of the birth of 'Tonight'.

What do they see as the secret of the Spinners' success? 'Bloody hard work,' says Jimmy, 'and all credit to them.'

The Spinners' television debut was casual. Tony, at that time (1961) still a teacher at Major Street Secondary Modern in Liverpool, got progressively annoyed as the pupils he taught got progressively listless. The root cause, he found, was too many late nights glued to the television screen.

So he penned a cautionary tale: 'Like my dad's cigarette and my ma's cup of tea, it's a terrible habit, this watching TV.' Within a few weeks he got a phone call from ABC Television ('We understand you've written a song knocking TV') and the Spinners were invited to sing it as a contribution to a debate on the evils of the expanding new medium.

The next year saw their first TV series, a host of radio spots, and Tony and Mick made their first trip to the States. All this before they'd even turned pro. In fact, the reason Cliff and Hughie couldn't go to America was because they couldn't get the time off work.

The trip was at the invitation of Pete Seeger, one of the fathers of the American folk song revival. Tony and Mick sang Liverpool songs like 'Maggie May' and 'Johnny Todd' in Greenwich Village. It was an experience neither of them was to forget . . . and one of the clinching factors which decided them to become full-time folk singers.

These early days were days of dreams and ambitions and 'flying balloons'. Beryl Davis remembers when the boys would come round to their home and sit and talk over coffee cups well into the night. 'Often they'd get a bright idea and Tony would be up and about to phone someone . . . before he realized it was two in the morning.'

They 'flew a balloon' over the BBC; suggesting a sixteen-week series of folk songs, based around the old sailors' recreation time, to be called 'Dance'n'Skylark'. And to lend it authenticity and a salt-tang they persuaded shanty-man Stan Hugill to agree to come each week with a song and a sea-tale to make it work. 'The format changed quite a bit between our "balloon flying" and the actual series,' Beryl adds. 'We had to compromise, but it was a start. It was a good start.'

'Dance'n'Skylark' was eventually produced in 1962 from the BBC's Dickenson Road studios in Manchester, which were housed in a converted church — a symbol perhaps of the faith the BBC had in the Spinners and the other artists who remember Dickenson Road with affection.

It was a natural thing for the Spinners to get themselves involved in sailing and singing shanties. All lived close to the ocean and Cliff had been born on an island. Their interest in ships and their involvement with sailing developed and broadened over the years — in Tony's case to representing Merseyside on the International Tall Ships Committee, and as a group to supporting the Ocean Youth Club.

So the Spinners asked to have Stan Hugill, the folk scene's foremost authority on sea shanties, as a regular when they appeared on 'Dance'n'Skylark'. In the series he was cast as the bosun with the boys as his crew, and each week a theme would be reflected in the guests they invited aboard.

Trevor Hill produced those first twelve 'Dance'n'Skylark' programmes. 'They were exciting to do,' he recalls. 'It was the first time we had staged authentic folk songs and sea shanties in what we hoped was a more or less accurate setting.'

There's no doubt the shows were expertly staged. The final set was a third of a full-sized boat, built in the studio (all the studio would actually hold), with cloud machines and real wet 'splashes' any time anyone fell overboard.

Young guests included the boys of Cheetham School for a Christmas edition, and Manchester YMCA for a pirate show. 'So realistic were the scars from the make-up department that one chap wore his home under his shirt, whipped it open to show his wife — and she fainted,' says Trevor.

Another hazard lay in Stan Hugill remembering *not* to sing the versions of sea shanties he used when singing in the folk clubs. 'Many a time he'd begin one, and halfway through say "Bloody hell, I can't sing that . . .", and we'd have to start again.'

The shows were an ambitious mix of song and dance, with choreography by Douggie Squires and a small orchestra led by Harry Hayward. The Spinners also did radio shows and charity work with Trevor over the years, and he has fond memories of their association and generosity. But in one vital aspect of their work he was proved wrong. 'I'm afraid I was one of those who counselled against them turning professional,' he confesses. 'How wrong can you be?'

The Spinners had first met Stan Hugill at a Fritz Spiegl Scouse folk concert at the Bluecoat Chambers in Liverpool. Stan is an acknowledged expert on the days of sail and sea songs and has written what are acknowledged to be the standard works on the subject. Fred Wood, when editor of *Folk Review*, once called him 'a singer of bluff enthusiasm'. He is also, as 'Dance'n'Skylark' was to show, an almost unstoppable raconteur.

'Every week, Stan would tell a sea story and such are the ways of television, he would be told to make it no more than two and a half minutes,' says Mick. 'Well, that was pretty near impossible for Stan, and invariably the floor manager would end up with more than he needed and have to edit it for the programme. But that wouldn't be the end of it. After the programme we would bring him back to Liverpool with us to appear at the club, and he'd still be continuing this story in the van. He had the most amazing tales of trips he'd been on and characters he'd met.'

Tony included a beautiful lilting love song from Newfoundland, 'She's Like the Swallow', in one of the programmes, and the producer was pondering ways to present it. 'I know,' he said. 'Swallows . . . birds . . . I'll get a pigeon!' So the BBC brought in a pigeon trainer and at the appropriate moment the bird was supposed to fly out and perch on Tony's shoulder. It did anything but, until the recording when it did it first time — to everyone's surprise.

'But the biggest surprise had been the producer's original train of thought — swallow . . . bird . . . pigeon! Funny ideas some of these television producers get!' says Mick.

On another occasion, the Spinners were booked to appear on a 'Woman's Hour' at BBC Manchester, and Cliff was due to sing 'Woman Sweeter than Man', part of the lyric of which goes 'I like coffee and tea, I like plenty whisky . . .' The producer however assured the boys they couldn't sing about whisky, not on 'Woman's Hour', and would they please change the lyric to something more

Entertaining children (above) *at Queen's Park School, Lincoln, where Cliff is a governor, and* (below) *at Windsor Street Primary School in Toxteth, just before a 1979 BBC radio series*

With Burl Ives, before their concert together in 1979 at the Liverpool Philharmonic Hall

A 1981 picture of Lonnie Donegan and Mick, once secretary of Lonnie's Liverpool folk and skiffle club

innocuous. 'I never knew if he was in fact getting at me or the song,' adds Cliff.

But they obliged — then, when they listened to the programme, heard before their spot a detailed report on prostitution, and after it an equally harrowing item on abortion. 'We looked at each other in amazement,' said Mick. 'To think we couldn't even mention whisky. Thank goodness things are a lot different now.'

They got their own back on the BBC however when they did a 'Tonight in Person' show from the Albert Hall, Bolton. Cliff was again rehearsing a quiet love song to include in the programme and as he sang it he was supposed to move through the audience which would be seated at little tables and serenade the ladies.

So the BBC producer came up to Mick and Tony and said, 'Are there any black women coming in tonight?' Both of them said 'How should we know? Why?'

'Well,' said the producer, 'we can't have Cliff singing this love song to a white girl. Can he bring his wife along?' When he was told Cliff's wife Janet was a Scottish lass, he became even more panicky.

Mick and Tony were enjoying the situation hugely by this time and tagged him along, till one or the other had a bright idea:

'Of course, Cliff does have a daughter . . .'

'That's it,' says the producer. 'Great. Great' So a taxi was organized to pick Lynne up from Liverpool and drive her over to Bolton, all so Cliff could sing this love song to her in the show.

'If it hadn't been our big chance, we might have told him where to go — and probably should have anyway,' says Mick. 'But the whole thing was really crazy. Miscegenation wasn't allowed — but incest was. Where's the sense in that?'

It was on that same 'Tonight' show that Hughie and Mick were sharing a hidden mike, which was taped to a pillar to pick up their guitars. But with the heat of the lights during the recording it began to wilt and drop even nearer to the floor. So the floor manager ended up crawling across to hold it up by hand, trying to keep out of shot at the same time. But despite the hitches, however, the Spinners must have made an impression, for they were quickly booked for 'A Spoonful of Sugar' and later for their own series from the Octagon Theatre, Bolton.

The Spinners big break came after they'd been interviewed on 'Woman's Hour' by Michael Barton, then working at BBC Manchester, and head of the BBC's local radio station network since 1980. When he heard that producer John Ammonds had been given a barn dance series to get together, and was looking for folk singers, he rushed along the corridors of BBC power and persuaded John to hear the Spinners.

So the boys were summoned and truly thought they'd blown it when they saw Ammonds turn away for a conversation with his secretary during their audition. But when they'd finished they were offered not only a show, but the whole series of six programmes. And that eventually grew into three series . . .

'We've never been short of media exposure; we've done regular radio and television shows because producers will always use us. They know the public are going to like us. But I sometimes feel this predictable approach has maybe worked against us — it hasn't encouraged us to do anything different, or producers to do different things with us,' thinks Mick. But it is this same consistency and familiarity which has brought them regular broadcasting work over the years. And in the beginning it was newcomer Hughie's infectious enthusiasm which got them on the air.

He was still exploring his own potential and the group was still basically a collection of solo singers with little but their enthusiasm going for them, when they applied for a BBC audition, and were accepted for radio's Guitar Club. Hughie went along to accompany the others on their set pieces, but nothing seemed to click for producer Jimmy Grant. Eventually he pointed at Hughie and said, 'What can he do?' Hughie at once extemporized his 'Talking Football Pools' and it went down a storm. He was booked to repeat it for the next broadcast — thus become the first Spinner to go on the air.

And, of course, in those days the Spinners were not as immediately recognizable as they were to become. BBC sports producer Nick Hunter remembers 'A Spoonful of Sugar' programme, in which young patients at Alder Hey hospital, Liverpool, asked to meet the Spinners.

'I must admit, my first thought in those days was of cricketers, Jim Laker and Tony Lock,' he admits.

Those Spinners' television series which most people remember best were the ones they did for the BBC from the Octagon at Bolton, because they combined good singable songs with equally good clean knockabout fun.

The first Octagon series was broadcast in 1968-9, produced by Nick Hunter, and with guests like Marie Griffiths from Wales, Ethne Campbell from Ulster — and a young Marti Webb, fresh from her success in *Oliver*!

To finish the first series, the Spinners invited Tony Murphy, who wrote their first best-selling single 'The Orange and The Green', and a group of children from a Liverpool school, trained by Diane Swindlehurst and calling themselves the Swindle Folk. These made such an impression that they eventually made a record.

The second Octagon series featured location inserts, masterminded by Barry Bevins, who was to become the Spinners' regular TV producer at BBC Manchester. They recorded a Scottish song with Cliff dressed up in a Black Watch kilt (what else?), and they all went tossing balsa wood cabers around the braesides and sword-dancing on rubber swords. They also did the 'Harriers' song, dressed up in running gear with Mick as timekeeper outside a country pub, swiftly getting more and more paralytic as the race wore on . . .

Guests began to be drawn from a wider field — Lulu, Sandie Shaw, Françoise Hardy, the tragic Sandy Denny, Acker Bilk, Moira Anderson, Julie Felix, George Chisholm and Esther Ofarim.

And as the shows caught on, their location work became more ambitious too, being filmed in the Lakes, in Cornwall, at Aldershot, as well as their Liverpool home.

When the Spinners invaded Aldershot, they got the Army to sing 'Family of Man' and Ed McCurdy's haunting

'Last Night I Had the Strangest Dream'.

'It was quite tremendous to hear the men singing out with gusto,' said Tony. 'I don't know if they meant it — the ranks might have, but I can't vouch for the officers.'

This was Mick's first encounter with the military mind, and quite an eye-opener. Producer Barry Bevins set up a shot which would show the Spinners being drilled with a small company on the parade ground, and the RSM appeared to do his stuff.

'Everything all right?' he asked Barry.

'Well, um, no,' said Barry. And he pointed to the far end of the parade ground where a corporal was putting a few men through some punishment drill — right in the line of camera shot.

'It would be nice if you could persuade them to move,' he suggested.

Without a second's pause, the RSM bellowed, *'Corporal, get that — — — — filth off my parade ground!'*

Mick was horrified, and turned to Hughie who, like Tony, had been in the Army for his National Service. 'But they're people,' he protested.

'They're not people,' said Hughie. 'They're soldiers.'

The Aldershot experience, however, produced perhaps the most memorable sequences from that series, which included Hughie singing 'The Banks of the Sweet Primrose' while walking through a training ground with explosions going off around him and tanks roaring past. As he sang this sweet lilting song, he became ever more muddy and dishevelled till, in the final shot, he was shown lying face down in the mud with caterpillar tracks imprinted across his back.

While the Spinners have been generally fortunate in securing regular television work, they have been less than fortunate with the times of day that it has been screened. The BBC tends to put out Spinners' programmes late in the evening, while ITV favours lunch-times — both odd choices to reach the family audience who enjoy the Spinners' kind of music.

Television brings other problems, as well. Being filmed at Liverpool's Pier Head for their 1970 BBC series, Tony was told the sweater he'd turned up in was too dark, and would he please change. He didn't have another with him, so there had to be a quick dash to the shops. And, being six foot seven, off-the-peg sweaters in his size are not that easy to find . . . frantic searching unearthed a pale blue cable-knit job that filled the bill, in just the nick of time before the light went completely.

Then there was the day that they were filming on location near Wigan, and a woman came along, walking her dog, innocently unaware that she was going to be in shot any second and spoil Tony's big entrance. There was only one thing for it — he'd have to tell her to move. He stepped from behind the tree which was hiding him, completely forgetting that he was in an animal costume. The woman took one horrified look at the giant fox looming towards her then — along with her equally startled dog — she fled.

The Spinners have never done a series from Liverpool, although the city has been used on more than one occasion for location work. They have performed the Liverpool barrowboys' song outside Lewis's store, and done 'Black and White' in a school playground in Violet Street, Liverpool 8. And from the old Shakespeare theatre, they did an international show with Chinese, French, Spanish, Scandinavians, Italians, Nigerians all singing a chorus of 'Everybody Loves Saturday Night' in their native tongues. (The Shakespeare burnt to the ground some months after this show — an ironic fact not lost on some Spinners' fans, who recalled disastrous fires at Butlins in Pwllheli and on board the *Moby Dick* at Blackpool, both after the Spinners had recorded there!)

Location work for the BBC dried up in the early 1970s, although the Spinners continued to do regular BBC series — either at Oldham or the Crucible, Sheffield, as well as their traditional Christmas specials in a variety of places. It wasn't until they signed for a series with Border TV in 1980 that they were location filming again. It was their first ITV series, and a huge success.

As well as television, the Spinners have done regular radio series for many years as well, the latest being The Spinners and Friends. Guests on this continuing radio series have included George Chisholm, Moira Anderson, Tom O'Connor, Acker Bilk, Lonnie Donegan, Isla St Clair, Dave Swarbrick, and Donald Swann. 'It is always a lot of fun — anything can happen, and usually does,' says George Chisholm. A frequent guest artist with the Spinners, he added his inimitable trombone playing to 'When the Old Dun Cow Caught Fire' on their *Not Quite Folk* album. Chisholm, noted for his sense of fun, greatly enjoys appearing with them: 'They are complete extroverts, yet underneath it all everything is always well organized. Spinners dates are always easy to do, meant to be enjoyed.'

Putting their courage and their love of the sea to the test, the Spinners joined the Ocean Youth Club in 1978 for the Tall Ships Race to Norway. Each joined a different ketch out of Great Yarmouth, and wives Beryl Davis and Chris Jones joined up as well. Cliff, definitely the least enthusiastic sailor of them all, got his sea-legs surprisingly quickly and busied himself in the galley for much of the trip, concocting West Indian dishes for his crew. They rewarded him by making him the first of the Spinners contingent to reach Oslo.

Cliff confesses he was scared at times, especially riding out those force seven gales. But he determined, for the good of the young crew, not to show he was scared. And it pleased him no end to be first home. 'I stepped ashore thinking, "Who's the sailor now?" and promptly fell over. My legs just went from under me. It took time to get used to standing on dry land again.'

Yorkshire TV made a film of the trip, which had had its frightening moments but even those gales and finding himself keeled over at forty-five degrees didn't dampen Tony's enthusiasm. He now has his own boat on Windermere, where he and Beryl go to relax and to get away from it all.

Hughie, too, has developed an interest in sailing — he has a holiday home, with moorings, in Wales on the Menai Straits — but his passion are the old sailing ships and windjammers, and he's thrilled that the Tall Ships are coming into Liverpool in 1984, and thrilled that Liverpool now has a Maritime Museum in the making.

He became obsessed for a time with the *Marco Polo*, pride of the old Black Ball line and a record breaker for the Liverpool to Australia run. He determined to write a ballad praising her achievement, and did his research well — writing to Lloyds of London, to the National Maritime Museum in Greenwich and then in a Liverpool pub he found a beer-mat giving a summary of all the information he needed: where and when she was built, the name of her skipper, the record she captured — the lot!

There's nowt so queer as folk

So what is a folk song — and does it matter? Many earnest performers, many erudite bodies have their own definitions, some contrived, some brief, some confused, some banal. (Sydney Carter dissuaded me from entering this particular debate, calling it a 'veritable minefield', and I was reminded of Louis Armstrong's definition of jazz which was always said to be: 'My idea of how a tune should go.')

Folk music was always there. The music of the common man, reflecting his feelings, his ambitions, his realities, it was a link with the past and a pointer to the future. Earnest enthusiasts have collected folk songs for ages, in the belief that one day those songs could be lost in the mists and myths of time. Such men of little faith failed to grasp the essence of the folk tradition — for folk is the music of survival, essentially underground, grass-roots music, surfacing joyfully now and then to show new generations that it is alive and the message it bears is always relevant. But to be worth singing a folk song has to have stamp of the common man about it. Folk music is a mongrel creation, taking threads from various melodic traditions over the centuries — even continuing that process today in the electric folk phenomena of the 1980s.

People have been saying for most of this century that folk songs and sea shanties should be collected before they die away, before the last memories of them fade. But in committing them to print, they then become frozen in time, so that they take on the form of holy writ. In attempting to 'rescue' songs, and yet to present them so that they would be suitable for family entertainment, it could be argued that folk song chroniclers and collectors, like Cecil Sharp or more particularly the earnest country clergymen of Victorian times, such as the Reverend Sabine Baring-Gould, bowdlerized lyrics to make them suitable for sensitive cultured ears. Now, purists will often accept no version other than that which they believe to be the original, and 'bastardized' lyrics are frowned on.

Does antiquity have to be an essential ingredient in a folk song — if so, what about the songs that are still being written today? Do they stay in limbo before being declared of the right vintage to qualify?

Copyright laws have added to the muddle also. It's no longer enough for a group to hear a tune and its lyrics, say 'That sounds good', and record it without reference — or reprisals.

So where does that leave traditional songs? Well, most have been copyrighted in the version and the arrangement in which they were collected, which puts considerable restriction on their use.

In practice lots of blind eyes are turned — but there are limits. Never again will there be that happy state where folk songs are free and for the common man. It's ironic to think that many of these songs sang hopefully of freedom and the loosening of shackles binding slave to master, worker to boss. Now, those very songs are shackled by the exigencies of modern copyright laws and recordings.

A well-remembered incident involves an aspiring folk-singer visiting a folk club in Liverpool, and part way through his spot, saying: 'I'd like to sing you a song I've just written...' then launch into Tony Davis's 'The Lure of TV'.

Two girls in the audience who were Spinners' club regulars were quick to spot it, and shouted out, 'That's not your song. Tony Davis wrote that song!' The singer stopped in mid-verse, and insisted, 'But it's mine. I wrote it only recently.' By now the girls had been joined by the club owner, who also recognized the song. 'It's on record, and

Tony's sung it on TV — that's what he wrote it for. You can't fool us,' the singer was told.

'So that's what's happening,' Tony explains now. 'Things are much more tightly nailed down. It means that perhaps no more traditional songs are going to appear in the future. There'll be far fewer "new" folk songs.'

But folk is definitely the music of survival, and this was demonstrated in a BBC documentary on its revival, 'The Other Music', broadcast in 1981. Folk reflects our history and our feelings, but it took an American to awaken the average Briton to his folk heritage. Alan Lomax, who had become interested in the authentic songs of the American pioneer, found a greater wealth of words and music in Britain. The paradox was not lost on the late A. L. Lloyd, who had also been chronicling and promoting British folk — as an antidote to the American swamping of our culture in the 1950s by rock, skiffle and blues.

With Ewan MacColl, Lloyd was aware of the industrial ballads and sea shanties which reflected grim times past as well as the triumphs of a former age. 'We had to convince people that we had a tradition as realistic, vigorous and vital as America at its best,' he explained.

Folk clubs mushroomed over Britain in the late 1950s and through the 1960s. The Spinners' club was one of the first outside London, but more than a thousand had been established by 1969. Protest lobbies like CND used folk as their music of demonstration and revolt, it was the music of the age, the music of the people. But folk was to have a lasting, deeper function than just protest. Alan Lomax spoke of 'opening up communication channels', Leon Rosselson of 'bringing people together', but he also noted sadly that many folk clubs had not reflected changes in the outside world.

Martin Carthy explains that the great strength of the folk club scene was the opportunity it gave to people to sing songs for other people without pressures. But the big weakness lies in many clubs having become 'flabby and constipated'. 'Folk clubs are the best thing we've got. They are our roots. We should use them,' he believes.

The folk scene *is* changing, and not always for the better.

How does the old guard see this change? A. L. Lloyd told viewers: 'Whatever enriches it is good, whatever impoverishes it is bad.' Others, like Frankie Armstrong, see the passion going out of folk as the skills improve. Modern recording techniques and sophistication have submerged the commitment, the guts, the conscience of folk.

Electric folk, exciting as it may be, hones the rough edges and loses some of the imagination of traditional folk. More and more artists are realizing the importance of maintaining contact with folk roots through the clubs instead of singing at audiences in a concert hall.

'Real folk music, as far as I'm concerned,' says Tony Davis, sticking his neck out, 'is traditional music performed by traditional singers, field singers. It's a very narrow definition but the only one that's unarguable. A song whose origins no one can trace, sung by a comparatively unlettered rural person is unarguably a folk song. It has been worked on by the communal process, been passed on and enjoyed by generations.

'And I know what are not folk songs, and they are the modern navel-contemplating dirges composed by would-be poets and some good poets too. Bob Dylan has a good deal of talent, and writes nice songs and sings them well, but nothing he produces can in any way be called folk.

'Between those two poles is however a vast grey area of compositions that are arguably folk music to some extent or other. If a song is sung the way its composer meant it to be sung, it is written down, it is scored and it is a composition. It is not a folk song. If, however, it has been passed on by word of mouth, misheard slightly, changed to suit the singer and his surroundings, yet retains its essential tune and gist, other pundits would say this gives it a folk purity, because it has been worked on by the communal process. It has the spirit of the people in it.

'The trouble today is that a songwriter writes a song down and with all the methods of mechanical reproduction a song is either printed or recorded almost as soon as it is written. It is solidified — it is there. There is a tale of an old woman once saying to Sir Walter Scott, who was writing down the songs as she was singing them, "None of my songs have appeared in print before. Now you're doing that I feel they're dead, they're frozen for ever."'

There are pros and cons to writing a song down. Whether in seemingly doing good, Cecil Sharp and the other collectors actually did harm to folk music is a moot point. What is certain is that in print the songs gain a wider dissemination than they would by word of mouth.

But what if the composer feels he wants to alter his original composition, which is already in print and been learnt in that form for some time? It annoyed Sydney Carter, author of 'Lord of the Dance', that the chorus had crystallized in print as 'Dance, dance, wherever you may be ...' when he eventually came to the conclusion that 'Dance, *then*, wherever you may be ...' sounded a lot better. A subtle change, but in his mind a vital one. He is now constantly irritated by schoolchildren who insist on singing what to him is the wrong version just because they have been taught it that way in school.

'I love folk, but wouldn't claim to write folk songs,' he says. 'Yet folk is more real to me than any other kind of music.' Carter calls himself a 'performing writer' and therefore has never written a song he couldn't sing himself. 'I write songs for myself. If other people wish to sing them, that's a bonus.'

Of Sydney Carter's songs Tony says: 'They have a sophistication, but also a folk feel about them. Some of what he has written is pure music hall, other is light cabaret stuff which suited Flanders and Swann well, and the rest might well be called "folk" one day. At any rate they've been accepted by the folk song world. But Sydney is not a man of the people and that is why sometimes his critics are suspicious of him. He is a very sophisticated intellectual who thinks and cares deeply about all manner of things.'

What about the argument that if a song is not written down it may be lost forever in a few generations? They have been saying that of sea shanties for years — and still new variants keep popping up, still Stan Hugill keeps adding to his repertoire, still 'new' folk songs keep appearing from the memories of West Country gypsies or

East Anglian farm workers or Scottish crofters or whatever.

'I get a little bit angry when people say to me, "You're singing it wrong," ' says Tony, 'when they mean you're not singing it as collected. If someone says I'm singing so and so's version of this song, I suppose that's all right. If they say I learnt it from so and so, and I'm doing it my way, that's better.'

The people who do folk the greatest disservice are those who make folk dull and boring. 'Real genuine traditional music sung by the field singers is fascinating,' adds Tony. 'Fred Jordon isn't boring — he's real, and he's a ham, and every nuance of expression lives. Jeannie Robertson, too, the queen of the ballad singers, wasn't dull and boring. She was incredibly entertaining. When she came to the club with an escort, she'd maybe be persuaded to sing three or four of those long ballads in a set, then have a rest, and come back with two or three more. If you're not used to them, they can be a bit overpowering. One may be fine, two tolerable, but after the third, you could see the audience fidgeting and saying to themselves: "Well, the Spinners reckon she's great so we'd better be respectful to her, but by God that old woman is driving me crazy!"

'But when Jeannie came to our club on her own, she said, "You'll be wanting me to do the ballads?" We said to her, "Jeannie, we wouldn't presume to tell you what to do. Do your own thing." So she began with a jolly chorus song, a short song, a joke or two, and then after ten or fifteen minutes when she had the audience eating out of her hand, she hit them with "Lord Donald" and they listened in awe, and when it was over, they went bananas. Not because we'd told them Jeannie Robertson was great and they ought to listen and applaud. Jeannie did that herself — because she was a natural entertainer, a great ham.'

Tony and the others recall going to a folk club and finding the resident band droning on drearily, in unnatural and phoney poses getting nowhere, then introducing the guests for the night. On this particular occasion they were three Americans, who socked it to the audience with a jolly set of knockabout stuff, some vaudeville material, some lively traditional songs, great variety.

'So I thought,' says Tony, 'these boys will have learnt something after the interval, the tone will lighten somewhat if they've any sense. But no — it was a quick "thank you very much" and back to a dose of the dirges. I don't understand this boredom bit. Some groups have got it into their heads that it's bad to be entertaining — that's what the Spinners do, and the Dubliners do, and the Corries do, but we mustn't do that. We must keep ourselves pure, and dull, and boring.'

So how does he and the rest of the group classify the Spinners? 'I call us bridge singers because we're the bridge between those who know nothing about folk music and the traditionalists. I want them to come and listen to us, hear what we do, and then go away and listen to the people we listen to. That's our aim — to get more people interested in the real and genuine traditional singers. But I don't want them to start off with us and move on to the phonies — unfortunately that happens too often. It's pretentious phonies who are strangling folk today.'

The Spinners' repertoire in early days was an amalgam of songs learnt at school or half remembered from sitting at grandmother's knee — or more often from listening to Leslie Howarth and researching in the library at Cecil Sharp House.

Cliff was encouraged to search the deepest recesses of his memory, and came up with 'Linstead Market', 'Matty Rag' and other childhood Caribbean lyrics.

Mick remembers going to a party with Cliff when he'd got the song collecting bug and spending the night lying on the floor listening to old scratchy 78s of Jamaican tunes on the record player. Cliff would say 'I know that song' (it might be 'Adam in the Garden') then when he hummed the tune to Jacqui McDonald she would remember a Yorkshire Girl Guide version of it; so between them they would cobble together suitable lyrics for the group. And there was a bohemian barber's shop in Liverpool 8 where Cliff lived, and it had a guitar hanging on the wall — anyone sitting around in there waiting for a trim or just killing time might get the guitar down and strum a tune.

Cliff would hear snippets of songs there that would strike a familiar chord and fill in the rest of the words from his memory.

Inside every reserved Englishman there's a ribald balladeer struggling to get out — at least that's Mick's theory, based on his experiences of staff parties in his teaching days. Working at St Francis Xavier's he met some Irish Catholic teachers who, when they were nicely primed with Guinness, would come out with spell-binding monologues and songs. 'But ask them in all sobriety to repeat it next day, or put a tape recorder in front of them, and they'd dry up,' he says. 'The circumstances had to be right — and of course in those sort of circumstances, the last thing you think about is tape recorders — or even pen and paper.

'That, to me, remains part of the mystery of the folk process — how these things are passed on from generation to generation. I found the whole thing quite incredible.'

Over the years the Spinners have added to their repertoire and amended the way they present folk to an audience whose appreciation and acceptance of folk has also changed. They have even produced songs themselves — Hughie particularly has written several fine ballads. Whether they will ever be accepted as 'folk songs' is debatable and doesn't worry him in the slightest. But he was quite pleased when one about the Ellan Vannin Tragedy was recorded by a Manx band called Kelly's Men who described it as a 'traditional song'. 'Most people who hear it now don't know who wrote it, let alone that I wrote it. And that doesn't bother me. It's really quite good, to think it's been accepted that way.'

So have the Spinners diluted folk by making it palatable to a mass audience? Stan Francis says it depends how you view it — 'It's like Lord Bath opening Longleat to thousands of people. That's "diluting", if you like, to have thousands tramping round your home. On the other hand he probably can't afford not to. Over-exposure dilutes anything, but you can't keep it locked away if others want to see it. The Spinners, by throwing open the doors of folk music, have probably exposed it for the general good. They must have broadened a lot of people's appreciation.

'What is more important is that they've encouraged participation. Going to watch football at Anfield or Goodison is totally different to watching it on the box. Going fishing with your rod in the rain is totally different to reading about it in a magazine. Going to watch the Spinners play in their club or at the Phil is an infinitely preferable experience than simply playing their records at home. And they've always made themselves available to their public.'

The Spinners have indeed remained one of the most approachable of the groups on the entertainment scene.

Has folk been over-exposed, and has it suffered? Stan Francis reckons 'popular' folk songs lose their appeal because they get hammered into pupils at school by well-meaning music teachers or turn up in every other folk singer's repertoire. 'They were probably collected at one time by Cecil Sharp or one of his contemporaries. Now every old man in an obscure rural corner of Britain is being dredged for songs of his youth, in the name of purity. Yet if they've been considered of sufficient merit to be perpetuated by someone learning them because of their interesting words or tune, they will survive.'

Sydney Carter has known the Spinners from Troubadour days 'when I used to feed them cornflakes and bananas', and known Donald Swann longer, since wartime when they were both in the Friends' Ambulance Unit (both being Quakers and conscientious objectors).

And in the Spinners in turn Donald Swann and his partner Michael Flanders found kindred spirits. 'We shared the same view of life and the world, one world, the family of man. The Spinners have made an important contribution to harmony.

'At the heart of folk culture,' adds Swann, 'is that belief that man is essentially himself. He may have something to say, or the talent to write beautiful lyrics but he is simply himself. When you turn professional, you lose nothing if you retain your sincerity. Whether you veer to the left or you veer to the right, the really sincere person remains essentially himself.'

Folk at the Phil: a view from the 'choirstalls' in the early days, with Bill Brown on bass, and a more recent shot from the auditorium, showing John McCormick

Sydney Carter, folk poet and songwriter (author of 'Lord of the Dance') with the Spinners

A Christmas cracker – Hughie in his 'Twelve Days of Christmas' outfit

Stan Hugill, who has known the Spinners since 1959, and in his words 'sung, acted and played with them many times over the years' is equally emphatic. 'They have been enormously helpful to the folk world, by helping young people enjoy folk music. The audience for folk music today wouldn't be so large if it wasn't for the Spinners.'

Stan is an unashamed Spinners fan himself — 'They sing my songs' — and especially enjoys listening to Hughie's rendering of traditional ballads. 'They're very cosmopolitan, very broadminded, and very good ambassadors for folk music,' he concludes.

Why are certain members of the folk revival so suspicious of the Spinners' success? Ewan MacColl says it's all a matter of disciplines. 'The Spinners may say they give people a flavour of folk and lead them on to explore other aspects of the folk spectrum, but in my experience that isn't true. Spinners' fans mainly remain Spinners' fans. The Spinners fall into the pop/folk world. That's not a value judgement, and I don't say it's better or worse. It's just a different road to travel.

'Folk music *has* its constants — it's not just the music, it's the style and performance that counts. After all, a Beethoven Quartet is patently not a Beethoven Quartet if it's played on the maracas. Now, our folk music's characteristics are uniform, and it is melodic, not harmonic. Tradition should determine performance and it is clearly more difficult to create that clear constant line within a group. The Spinners are not alone in this — the Clancy Brothers and many other groups have travelled a similar road. So in Britain and in America we have made our own disciplines and ignored tradition to a certain extent. The result is a hotchpotch — interesting maybe, but still a hotchpotch.'

It's perhaps their extra ingredient of entertainment and outreach which has set the Spinners, and the Corries and the Dubliners, apart from the rest of the folk scene. Still, it is broad and exciting enough to accommodate many streams of enjoyment, narrow or broad. But there are anomalies, and they niggle.

'Take Martin Carthy,' says Tony. 'He is the idol of traditionalists. His singing is very fine, and his guitar playing, which I love, is essentially his own style. It is brilliant, but it has nothing to do with "traditional music". I don't see how traditionalists can justify praising Martin Carthy's excellent (but untraditional) guitar playing, yet reject Cliff Hall's equally fine and inimitable harmonica, which — I think — has more of the *feel* of folk tradition.'

'Of the four of us, Mick is the one who gets most upset by it all. I've learnt to shrug my shoulders and content myself with the thought that thousands still come to hear us, and get involved in folk music through us. As far as I'm concerned, that's reward enough.'

Cliff is even more phlegmatic. 'We do our own thing. It suits us and it makes us a lot of friends, and it makes a lot of people happy. So that must be all right.'

It is no accident that one of the Spinners' most popular albums (and there have been many) was called *Not Quite Folk*. It contained many fine songs in the folk idiom — but folk songs of the future? A combination of personal pride, copyright laws, and traditional stubbornness probably governs the answer to that.

Hughie again: 'In the old days I remember seminars that went on for whole weekends while people argued about the definitions of folk music. Everyone seemed to have a different idea. Bert (A. L.) Lloyd wrote the folk music section for the *Encyclopaedia Britannica*, and he says simply that a folk song is "a song that touches you". Others will say folk music stopped at a certain date. Perhaps they're all right in their different ways — I don't know. I do know a lot of breath has been wasted trying to thrash it out, and really it's not that important.

'What is important is the enjoyment folk music gives to millions.'

Who needs hits?

Chart success is something that has, surprisingly, eluded the Spinners. Although they have been consistent and very popular performers for twenty-five years they have achieved success without a Number One hit or a best-selling album. Their most popular singles — 'The Orange and the Green', 'Dirty Old Town', 'Black and White' — topped local charts, but missed national chart success for a number of reasons from postal strikes to regional bias.

This is something that particularly annoys Mick Groves. While the others have accepted the situation over the years and can rationalise it, Mick still gets uptight about record sales. 'I'll never understand how a group of our stature, having broken records for capacity houses in concert halls all over the country, and having done major regular and successful concert tours of Britain, haven't had that success reflected somewhere in the album or singles charts. Yet I can name you half a dozen other bands who haven't had our kind of success, and *are* regularly in the charts.'

That doesn't mean Spinners records do not sell — they sell consistently and they sell well. Their *Love is Teasing* album sold thirty thousand in two issues. But consistent sales do not make the charts — only massive sudden sales.

'It's only that fact, that we do sell records, that keeps me relatively quiet, but it does make me angry. I'd still love to crack this thing. I'd still love for us to have a Number One, not to further our career, not now — but just to say we've done it. Besides if you get a Number One you invariably get a follow-up, maybe a couple, and with the exposure that would give us, it would be enough to give us a job for life and a pension for life. It would also open up doors to us that have so far been closed — including the lucrative American market, maybe. It amazes me that we've done everything in this business — television, concert tours, cabaret — but never had that damned hit record.'

Reaching other people, new audiences, that's what it's all about. 'That's what doing television was all about — not furthering our career as such, but reaching as many people as possible. Now, if we got into the pop market with a hit record, we could reach a totally different section of the population, with a totally different kind of music — make them aware of folk, make it available to them.'

How to achieve chart-topping success has been as much a puzzle to the group's record producers over the years as it has been to the group. One producer reckoned it out — if the Spinners do a hundred concerts a year and get two thousand people at each (not impossible, in fact quite likely), that's 200,000 people they've reached in twelve months. But only one in ten will buy a Spinners record, and then not all at once, but in a steady sale over the year. So although the records are sold in good numbers, they seldom register in the fast-selling charts.

Other producers tell them, however, that they don't need a hit. The essence of the Spinners' success has lain in their intimate approach, even in the largest concert halls, to reaching an audience through a friendly stage presence. There's little a hit record could do to enhance their reputation ('"Lily the Pink" demolished the Scaffold,' mutters Tony darkly).

But lack of chart success does rankle. Way back in 1975, Mick was forecasting big things for the prize-winning 'Castles in the Air' — a European hit maybe. 'Look what hits did for Nana Mouskouri. It would be great to play a big European concert hall like she can. We can only do that with chart success.'

Is it a question of money? 'Not necessarily,' he added. 'Money we got. Recognition would be nice.'

'The maxim any performer lives by is to do what you do as well as you can — and keep going,' adds Tony, 'and using that yardstick the Spinners are a success. We have so many records on sale at any one time that we are never out of the record catalogues.'

Folk at the Phil was the title of their first big-selling LP, a live recording of refreshing spontaneity and zest. Several of the Spinners' albums have been recorded live. It gives them an added dimension, what John McCormick calls 'a raw folksy edge' — but they are hair-raising to do.

'It's very much a warts and all affair,' remarks John, 'especially if it's recorded at just one concert. I like the approach some record companies take where they record three live concerts and marry the best bits into one.' This was done with the Spinners' *All Day Singing* album, a favourite among their fans. But John still reckons concerts used as recording sessions are a bit unfair on the audience. 'Often it can interrupt the flow of a concert, especially if the recording engineers want a number repeated. It is the same if it's being recorded for television or radio, though you have the added bonus of knowing your reaction is going to add to other people's enjoyment.

Folk at the Phil was launched in April 1964, and at least three live LPs have come from successful Philharmonic concerts — the Christmas one is now a Liverpool tradition and there is generally another (maybe two) some time during the year.

Phil audiences must be among the most amenable anywhere.

The Spinners once even had to tell them all to keep a secret — in the programme notes Tony had let slip that the group would be taking part in 'A Spoonful of Sugar' broadcast from Alder Hey Children's Hospital in the city — and it wasn't until concert day that Mick spotted it and let out a howl.

'You idiot!' he said. 'That's meant to be a big surprise. The BBC will probably kill our contract if they or the children get to hear about it!' There was only one thing for it — take the whole audience into their confidence about this slip-up, cross their fingers and hope. On the day of the recording at Alder Hey, the Spinners arrived and were welcomed as unexpected guests.

The ruse had worked.

One nurse whispered to them as they passed down the corridor, 'See — I didn't tell a soul!' She'd been in the Phil that night and kept their secret — and so had hundreds of others.

In 1974 the Spinners played the London Palladium, and each has his own happy memories of that unforgettable night. Cliff calls it 'one of my dreams come true', and for record producer Peter R. Vince it was a special night too. It marked his first album with the Spinners and the start of a highly successful seven-year association with EMI. 'Live albums always have a certain magical quality about them,' he explains, 'and this one is possibly the most enjoyable of their live albums to listen to. In fact, we finished up with too much good stuff, and if I was asked which of their albums sums up the essential Spinners, I would pick that Palladium recording. It conjures up all that is good and entertaining about a Spinners' concert.'

Captured in studio conditions with all the advantages of modern recording technology, folk can sound too contrived and lose its appealing spontaneity, thinks Peter Vince. Yet another of his favourite Spinners albums was a studio production — their Christmas collection of twenty favourite Christmas carols. The Spinners were augmented on that collection with good session men — including guitarists Alan Parker and Kevin Peek, percussionist Brian Bennett, and Merseyside's own Bob Buckle on banjo. John McCormick's arrangements helped too. 'When you have someone good playing with you it helps you to lift your own playing too,' Peter Vince explains. 'That, for me, was the best produced album of our association.'

Disappointing singles sales over that period do not worry him, offset as they are by staunch and solid album sales. 'It is very rare to get a folk single into the charts, anyway,' he adds. 'Castles in the Air' he liked, but never saw as chart potential; 'Black and White' should have been a chart entry, but was prevented by a countrywide postal strike, hampering the all-important sales returns as well as distribution; and the Spinners' version of Tom Paxton's 'Last Thing on My Mind', although it stood out from the recording session as something special, and got loads of air-time on radio, never took off with the public.

'But it was a good seven years,' adds Peter. 'They were not always the easiest to get along with. As four individuals you couldn't meet nicer guys, but put them together... well, at times they really frightened me. Yet, strangely, it was this relationship which held them together all these years. I enjoyed the experience immensely and am only sorry not to be working with them any more. There's no denying they do work hard — hard enough to kill a younger group, let alone one that's getting on a bit ...'

The wheel has come full circle for the Spinners, now back with record producer Terry Brown, who produced their early albums for Fontana and is now producing their latest albums for the PRT group. How does he view the Spinners after all this time? 'Bloody marvellous, otherwise I wouldn't have wanted them back. As it is, they are still incredibly popular and I'm thrilled with them. They look a lot better fed these days and a little older of course, but basically they're still the same four blokes I got to know back in the 1960s.'

Even if they don't have hits in the charts, the Spinners continue to attract people to their club. What is the appeal of folk nights with the Spinners? A *Liverpool Echo* writer, the late Howard Channon, came closest to distilling that unique atmosphere into words when he wrote a four-part 'Focus on the Spinners' in 1970.

They were then still performing at the now-demolished Gregson's Well, and Channon marvelled at the way the audience volume would threaten to split the low ceiling one minute with 'Whip Jamboree', yet be 'chapel quiet' the next to listen to Cliff's gentle rendering of 'Come Back Liza','his lullaby fingers caressing the strings'.

Channon found himself sandwiched at the bar between the sort of Liverpool characters more recently epitomized by Alan Bleasdale in 'Boys from the Blackstuff'. There were the Jacques brothers, Tony, Jimmy and Brian, 'ex-dockers with Herculean shoulders and much hair on their cheeks', and Tony Wilson 'enormously ginger-bearded, wearing an old railwayman's peaked cap and a reefer jacket with nautical buttons, the general effect being of a shellback come ashore from a windjammer'.

Hughie and Chris knew Tony Wilson, for he used to sing with Chris in the Bothy Band, and Hughie recalls the fate of that cap. 'Tony caught the steam bug and got that hat from Chris's dad. He wore it on one steam freaks' trip on board the *Royal Scot*, and lost it by sticking his head out of the window going over Shap. The wind blew it away. Undaunted, when he got to journey's end he rang the nearest signal box and asked if they'd found it. They said they had and he said, "Great, I'm on my way to pick it up." "Don't bother," they said. "We put it in the firebox to keep us warm."'

Channon reckoned the lot of them 'good company to keep when carrying a briefcase down one of those jowlers (alleys) off Wapping on a dark night'.

More his size were Tony Murphy, the genial writer of the Spinners' first really popular single, 'The Orange and The Green', and Stan Kelly, who wrote the equally popular 'I Wish I Was Back in Liverpool', as well as Stan Francis — all club regulars in those days. In fact Stan Francis would join the Jacques brothers and one or two others in a group they called the Liverpool Fishermen, giving out with their own brand of shanties and humour.

Nowadays at the Triton, if the characters are no longer larger than life (though the years do add exaggeration to any retelling of a favourite tale) the names still drop by, be it from the Everyman or the Playhouse, or the local folk scene.

The reasons why people go to folk clubs like the Triton, however, don't seem to change. One told Channon: 'I like folk best with a pint in my hand.' And the Spinners — they still go to the club because they enjoy it, because it keeps them in regular and intimate contact with 'the folk'.

While critics have carped at their style over the years, none can deny or fail to marvel at their staying power.

Liverpool Echo writer Joe Riley, marking their twenty-first anniversary in 1979, called them 'four mellow yellow songsters in mandarin collars and baggy trousers, giving the impression they're still living in the early 1960s'. Yet even he had to admit that while so many of their contemporaries had been blasted to oblivion by synthesizers and laser-sharp music, they had remained spinning their magic threads.

Back in 1968, *Liverpool Daily Post* critic Doreen Tanner was falling under their spell at the Playhouse. 'Theirs is a deceptively simple formula . . . Something new to say about the Spinners? Not really. They will discover new songs, new ways of putting them across, but basically they have remained miraculously unchanged and unspoilt. Their fans would not wish it otherwise. Familiarity is half the enjoyment.'

Television critic H. Wason Ross, writing on their 1971 series from the Octagon, was among those who praised the fact that listeners could follow a Spinners' lyric, unlike some Top Ten chartbusters of the time.

And Howard Channon, at one of the many Christmas at the Phil concerts — this one in 1974 — recorded Tony actually finding someone in the stalls who wasn't singing. 'You're not — a Southerner, are you?' he asked in shocked tones. It was not so much a Christmas concert, more a Christmas party.

The Spinners have never done a summer season or a panto — 'We'd probably drive ourselves round the bend if we tried,' says Mick frankly. 'Being that close and doing the same thing night after night would probably bore us. It's not the way we operate.'

'Doing the same thing in the same place night after night for something like eight or ten weeks I'm sure would become false after a while,' reckons Cliff. 'I feel my heart wouldn't be in it. Once it starts just being a job, being repetitious, the fun is gone.'

'On the road,' explains Mick, 'Tony might change the programme halfway through a tour, just to keep us fresh, for what we do needs to be spontaneous to work. It's almost an amateur approach to putting on a show, and some people in show business don't rate us because of that. But over the years we've polished what we do, and we can change what we do without losing that polish, while at the same time keeping that important element of spontaneity.'

The element of fun, of spontaneity has led the Spinners to festoon their guitars in folk artist tradition with a number of stickers, espousing certain causes (CND, War on Want, Manchester United FC) or just fun slogans ('Jesus Saves — but St John Scores'). Nowadays they even have woolly mascots, made or given by grateful fans, hanging from the guitar frets.

Fans are always quick to pick up on any chance remark. In the early days the only Welsh song the boys knew was 'Cosher Bailey'; it is recorded on the LP *More Folk From the Phil*, with the audience obviously having much fun making up verses. Sung in 'pidgin Welsh', one of the many and varied verses referred to 'mochyn du' which Tony had to explain meant 'black pig'. This prompted Cliff, whenever Tony said it, to leap in with a swift 'Watch it!' It wasn't long, therefore, before Cliff began getting 'mochyn du' stickers and so on with which to adorn his guitar.

But nothing caused so much comment and consternation as the Secret of ROMFT. Mick was given a ROMFT sticker after a concert for naval ratings at Rothsay, and it stood for (so they were told), 'Roll on my final twelve', alluding to the end of a sailor's term of duty. Spinners' fans being Spinners' fans, however, more racey interpretations began circulating, a favourite being 'Roll on Mick's fat tum'. Fans outside the navy wrote in to criticize the Spinners for blatant advertising, believing ROMFT to be a new make of super-guitar, and ex-naval types wrote in to point out kindly that ROMFT had extremely rude connotations among those in the senior service.

It was fun while it lasted, but the joke wasn't prolonged. You could say the Spinners cleaned their act up in more ways than one when they discovered the Secret of ROMFT, and ditched it hastily. And when ROMFT disappeared, a number of the other stickers disappeared too.

Like most groups on the road in constant proximity to

each other, they have their rows; unlike some groups in similar circumstances they tend to get over them pretty quickly. A *Radio Times* feature in the mid-1970s suggested that the rows were violent and frequent, and anxious fans wrote in by the shoal to plead with the lads not to break up, to patch it up, to tell the truth . . .

The truth is evident. They could not have survived twenty-five years or more together without a cross word. But their family commitment to each other, to the group and to their fans is immensely strong and sufficient to overcome all danger of permanent damage.

Those rows can, however, still frighten those outside the family. Johnny Mack admits that when he first joined, he thought often that the Spinners were on the verge of splitting up.

'We can laugh about it now, but they scared me when I first walked into them. I suppose violent rows are the best in a way because they clear the air, and everyone settles back into a routine again. There's certainly no long-running feud, that is the killer with a lot of groups. There's no lasting bitterness.'

'Usually, when we're travelling,' explains Tony, 'the rows are over where we'll stop on the motorway for a cup of tea — that is always a source of friction. "We stopped there last time and the food was awful". Or "I don't feel like eating, I had a big breakfast anyway." And we have crazy arguments about things which are totally irrelevant, really. But I suppose it's better to let off steam like that than over anything important.'

'Mick says it's like a marriage,' adds Hughie. 'It would be silly to pretend we didn't fight. But we don't fight about the music. We have an affinity in our music which always draws us together again.'

'Everybody's bound to get uptight now and then,' says Cliff, 'but we cope with it very well, and when we finish work we each of us disappear home to our families and we relax.'

The Spinners made a conscious decision many years ago to take school holidays off — arising from the schoolteacher backgrounds of Mick and Tony maybe, but also sensible if they were to spend time with their children and enjoy them growing up.

Tony finds it a blessing even now. 'The others have still got children at school. But now my girls have left, I find Beryl and I can get away any time and go up to our boat on Windermere — not necessarily to sail but just to collapse for a day or two. There's no telephone on the boat, you see — that's the attraction. They can't get us on the boat!'

Communication chords

Buxton on a crisp autumn evening. Half an hour before curtain up at the ornate opera house (Mike Harding's venue for one of his TV series) and the Spinners are backstage. Mick is shaving, Hughie is puffing on his second cigar and Cliff is tuning up. All have changed into their stage uniform of open-collared yellow shirts with beaded necklaces, dark trousers and patent leather shoes.

In the next dressing room, however, Tony and Johnny are far from ready — both still in their travelling clothes, and eating. Tony has water biscuits covered in cottage cheese and jam; Johnny has coffee, lots of coffee to soothe his ulcer.

The fact that Tony is eating is probably good news for the others, otherwise he'd be bouncing around full of energy, eagerness and exhortation. It's his way of working himself up so he arrives on stage with the adrenalin nicely flowing.

Cliff, on the other hand, needs contemplation, almost a yoga-like preparation, and where possible likes a room to himself. At Buxton he had to be content with a corner, around which he erected his own forcefield, which it was unwise to penetrate.

Hughie, too, tends to be quiet, but he paces, getting the running order locked in his mind.

Only Mick is fully occupied, organizing the lighting and the sound people, making his own pre-concert check so that those concerned with its presentation are as in tune as the lads on stage.

'I know that while the others are being incredibly introverted, I'm usually running round doing last-minute things, sorting out tickets, little details, deadline panics ... it can be a bit annoying, and a bit noisy, but I can't help it,' pleads Tony. ('It's his nerves, you know,' says Cliff, with sympathy. 'We've got used to it over the years ... you have to.') He's also the only one of the four not to wear a beaded necklace, even though determined fans have sent him dozens over the years. 'It's just not my style,' he explains.

Only a matter of minutes before curtain up, and Tony starts to get changed. 'He's a last-minute man by nature,' explains John, as he downs the last of his coffee. 'A deadline man — that's his style.'

A packed house gives them a warm reception. They respond with 'Drunken Sailor' and 'Woman Sweeter than Man'. The lyrics are changed to 'Woman Sweeter than I' to rhyme with River Wye in deference to the location. Tony winces good-humouredly at the contorted words.

Hughie launches into his solo, 'Talking Football Pools'. 'It's dead easy to play — all on three chords, G, C and D ... that's the hard one, if you can't see the chalkmarks.'

Tony suddenly realizes the 'Royal' box contains a party of teenage girls and, nudging the rest of the group, does a sideways glance and a very correct bow. All follow suit on cue.

Hughie tells the joke of the Derbyshire poacher caught by the village policeman, and threatened with court proceedings. 'Have you ever seen a JP?' he asks. 'No,' says the poacher. 'But I once saw a barn owl sh — —!' So much for the family image.

(At the Colston Hall, Bristol, the week before, they'd soothed a tired and emotional heckler with a sparkling version of 'Shenandoah'. It did the trick in between a cracking Ken Dodd impersonation from Hughie and a rip-roaring 'Auntie Maggie's Remedy', in which Cliff sang 'I went to the doctor's, I didn't feel well ...' to be told by Mick, 'Yes, you're looking off-colour.' It was their very effective way of coping with the odd spot of trouble, but Buxton is well behaved.)

The tempo changes effortlessly to Mick introducing

Woody Guthrie's 'This Land is Your Land'. 'I wish someone would write a song about Britain as good as this one about the States,' he says.

Then, with the audience completely in the mood, it's back to the rumbustuous antics of 'Little Cottage in the Wood', with everyone encouraged to do imitations of 'Kung Fu rabbits', and the spotlight eventually falling on one of the boxes where one chap is spontaneously doing a marvellous job, and gets an equally spontaneous round of applause, led by the Spinners themselves. To round off this spot of nonsense, Mick and Hughie do their kindergarten version — 'To think he's 45 next week!' says Hughie.

Half time and more coffee, plus Buxton spa water for the stage. 'This is the first time we've been in the Opera House,' Tony says. 'We've been in the Glasshouse (Pavilion) next door but this is beautiful — just like being inside a wedding cake.' At the Pavilion the same night there is a wrestling bill and Cliff has been mistaken for the Mississippi Mauler, which amuses him greatly.

They pepper their act with songs from their latest album, signified by Harry Worth type raising of the right arm and leg ('Or if it's on the B side, the left arm and leg,' says Mick) to save them repeating 'And now from our latest album . . .' all through. Cliff hams up 'Coney Island Washboard Roundalay', Johnny does his 'Kick the Cat' solo, and they end with generous encores — the Maori version of 'Now is the Hour' ('We got the words off a tea towel'), 'Lord of the Dance', 'In my Liverpool Home'.

Backstage, afterwards, young and old queue gratefully for a word, an autograph, a last smile . . . and they're away.

A sunny day at Worsley Delph, on the outskirts of Salford. Opposite the Bridgewater Hotel, behind the old Court House, is the start of forty-six miles of historic canal workings, dating back to the eighteenth century and feeding the coal and iron ore mines in the area.

The Spinners are on location for a BBC documentary charting the building of these canals and their importance to Manchester and its trade. They are rehearsing ten new songs on a scaffold jetty jutting out into the cut, where the water is the colour of British Leyland's 'sandglow', the legacy of generations of iron ore mining and of flooding the iron ore workings, many years ago.

Families on gaily painted narrow boats with names like *Princess Anne* and *Lloyd George* brew their tea and listen to the history unfolding in song.

Over lunch at the Casserole the Spinners mull over the script. 'Which is Camera One?' asks Mick of producer Barry Bevins. Discussion of the lyrics of one song has Tony maintaining that Hughie and Mick sang the wrong words while he was the only one singing the right words. 'We won't sing the wrong words this afternoon, will we?' he says in his best schoolmaster's voice, a remark that will be remembered during the recording when Hughie and Mick sing the right words, but Tony goes wrong. Broad satisfied grins spread over their faces.

Mild horseplay at the lunch table. 'I'm not a complete fool,' Johnny suddenly says, to be told, 'You're doing a good impression then, chuck.'

Back at the cut, the BBC has taken over a convenient kitchen as dressing room and the make-up girl and wardrobe lady get a close-up of Tony's operation scar. 'Isn't that lovely — I'm made up with that!'

Cliff is the first away to practise on his own in peace and pick his autoharp. All of them have found it a strain to learn ten new songs for this recording, but perhaps Cliff even more than the others.

Back on the jetty the painters have been at work: Tony finds the green stool he's been using all morning is now red. Cliff lays out his harmonicas and worries in case they bounce off and disappear for ever beneath the murky waters.

Then the recording engineers ask them to change the red pullovers they are wearing as they are 'flaring' on the monitors. The boys choose a set of pale yellow cabled alternatives, knitted for them by an elderly friend in Sheffield. Mick unknowingly wears his inside-out all through the recording. It is only spotted when he moves from the jetty to record his solo.

It's a Celebrity Knock-Out: Mick takes a plunge, watched by Stuart Hall

Tony demonstrates how to sail a rubber dinghy and stay dry

'Dip and fall back' – unimpressed with Cliff's culinary skills during the making of a series for Border Television

Behind every great man: (left to right) *Chris Jones, Beryl Davis, Janet Hall, Margaret Groves*

The audience begins to arrive and a patient BBC cameraman is now engulfed by eager Polaroids and ambitious Nikons. He grins and steadies Camera One which now has shopping in Tesco carrier bags stacked around its wheels. Johnny pretends to dive off into the water; the women love it, and offer him sweets and kisses.

Into the recording, the producer asks the Spinners to do the opening number again. 'Of course,' says Tony. 'Practice makes perfect.' The producer agrees a little too readily, and Tony looks aggrieved. It was meant to be a joke.

'Did you know, they asked that chap to moor his boat over there?' says Hughie to the audience, pointing behind them. 'He said, "I can't do that. I've just seen a duck walking on the water!"'

Time is getting on and schoolchildren begin to walk through on their way home. Extremely patient BBC production team explain to them that running feet on tarmac sound like machine-gun bullets, and pray nobody waves at the camera.

After a series of fluffs and technical hitches, some on one side, some the other, Cliff forgets the words and gives a peace sign to the producer. 'The score is now BBC 6, Spinners 4.'

Then comes the naughty song, 'Boatie, boatie, spit in the cut and wipe your nose on a mop stick'. Tony insists these are the original words. 'If you know any variations, keep quiet.' Collapse of quartet on run-through when Mick sings 'Wipe your nose on a snot stick.' 'So much for the family image,' he reflects.

Mick then goes off to do a solo on board one of the boats. Cliff, visibly relaxed, chats with the children, while Tony thanks the audience and tells them of the probable transmission date.

That leaves Hughie nursing a stubbed toe and joking with the local bobby: 'Not much mass hysteria today, eh?'

A few months later and it's Yorkshire TV studios in Leeds, to record inserts for a 'Sunday Best' show with Frank Topping, and guest spots on a Harry Secombe special.

Lots of waiting around as the studio is set up, mikes positioned, run-throughs arranged, then recorded. There is no audience for these segments; their applause will be dubbed on later, so the boys acknowledge the cheers of a silent studio when they finish. It's eerie and the lack of feedback off-putting but the producer is pleased.

Cliff started the day in a less-than-perfect humour when it looked as if he'd been left to hump the gear to the dressing room alone while the others disappeared. Lack of communication between them and the studio crew seemed to be to blame. 'Man, these sort of hassles I can do without.'

His mood isn't improved by a missing pair of shoes. They're eventually located in a dressing-room cupboard. 'I thought I was doing you a favour,' pleads Hughie, falling victim to one of Cliff's special looks.

Meanwhile Mick tries to draw the others into a familiar topic. 'How many one-hit wonders can you name over the past ten years?'

The Spinners include their version of the lilting Welsh air 'Ar Lan y Mor' especially for Sir Harry, who joins them and Deryck Guyler on a pretend washboard with silver foil on his fingers instead of thimbles, for yet another 'Coney Island Roundalay.'

'That was lovely,' says the producer, encouragingly. 'Lovely?' retorts Harry. 'I've done nothing! I feel a right idiot, and me silver paper keeps dropping off.'

February 1982, and the fiftieth anniversary Folk Spectacular of the English Folk Dance and Song Society at the Royal Albert Hall. Massed morris men, clog dancers, Irish dancers, country dancers, children's favourites, concertina virtuoso Alistair Anderson, and the Spinners topping the bill.

In their element, they link the items, and for Maritime England Year take part in a special tableau of song and dance to celebrate Lord Nelson.

The anniversary also coincides with the centenary of the birth of Percy Grainger, so the afternoon and evening performances include a selection of his works too. A full programme to remember and perform — it's inevitable the odd hitch will occur. Hughie completely dries up during one of the Nelson songs to his immediate embarrassment, and despite a quick recap rehearsal in the dressing room beforehand.

But they get it together for the finale, which sees Johnny pretending to drink a pint of real ale, and playing the bass flat out on the floor during 'Come Landlord Fill the Flowing Bowl', and Cliff hamming it up marvellously as Old Mrs Flipper-Flopper in 'A Fox Went Out', while Mick attracts more than a few boos and hisses behind his fox mask.

The Albert Hall is alive with costumes and music and fun and celebration and the odd mistakes are accepted and forgiven. At the end the whole company join the Spinners with 'In My Liverpool Home' and the applause is deafening. Whoever said folk was dead?

Go on, then

How long can the Spinners go on? They are consistent crowd-pullers, their popularity seems as timeless as Cliff Richard's, and Tony sums up their attitude: 'We'll keep working as long as people want to see us.'

He would, however, like to see the number of venues they play each year decrease, concentrating on fewer concerts in larger halls, rather than spreading themselves over some of the smaller halls. 'But it's difficult — if people want us to come and entertain them, we find it very hard to refuse.'

Which is good news for their fans, who have never been deliberately short-changed by the Spinners. The group don't refer to them as 'the public, the punters, the peasants', as some artists do. 'We never forget, after all, that it's the fans who pay our wages,' explains Mick. Twenty-five years has developed a highly receptive attitude to what their fans want, and a rapport with their audience which is the envy of other performers.

Tony: 'There's a folk group from America, who were very big a few years back, and I had an LP of theirs which I used to rave about. So I went to see them when they came over and sat in the audience able to recite the whole of their act, ad libs and all, word for word. It was so rehearsed, it was no longer spontaneous. And it was a big let-down.'

'You always say that about the Clancy Brothers, don't you?' adds Hughie wickedly.

The Spinners are still passionately interested in Liverpool

and its future . . . feeling the Liver-pull of the river and the sea, and fostering the idea of an annual River Festival and the growth of the Maritime Museum, to remind people not only of the greatness of Liverpool's past, but to make people aware of the river and draw them together across it. A divide has grown up over the years between the people of the Wirral and the people of Liverpool, and it has not helped to eliminate the gulf by designating both sides of the river 'Merseyside' in local government boundary changes.

Many were ready to write off the old port of Liverpool some years ago as 'dead', when in fact its function and its role is changing. The Spinners are among those rooting for the future of a revised and revived Liverpool. 'It will take a while for the changes to be complete, for Merseyside to come alive again, but it's all happening,' believes Tony. He and the rest of the group feel encouraging grass roots support now for schemes like the Maritime Museum, the River Festival and the International Garden Festival, which transformed the South Docks into a riverside walkway and park. The Tall Ships came into Liverpool in 1984, racing from Quebec and from Stockholm round the north of Scotland, a mass of magnificent square-riggers converging on the Mersey once again. (But the face of the docks has been changed forever with the coming of the Seaforth container terminal. Where once the cargo ships which came into Liverpool disgorged their holds on to the quaysides and thousands of Liverpool dockers were needed to cope with the influx of world trade, now everything is transported in boxes. More freight may come into Liverpool these days, but the average Liverpudlian gets little benefit from it.)

Liverpool is, however, beginning to do something with its dockland heritage, bringing it back to life as a tourist attraction, and as a testimony to bygone prosperity. 'We can see Merseyside has a big future. It's not a case of looking out across the river and saying, "Wasn't it marvellous when . . ." but looking ahead and saying, "Won't it be marvellous when . . .". That's what we're really looking forward to,' adds Tony.

And what do the individual Spinners look forward to, saying 'Wont't it be marvellous when . . .'?

'If the Spinners pack up, I don't want to retire and do nothing,' says Tony. 'I want to have something else to do, something satisfying, a career. At the moment, however, I definitely don't want us to split. But we could cut down our group appearances and develop our individual interests to our advantage. I'm reaching the time when I'd like to improve my personal quality of life, spend more time with Beryl, do other things.

'There are hundreds of traditional English songs I would like to sing but don't get the chance to. We did a concert with the Royal Liverpool Philharmonic Orchestra recently and we learnt "Blow Away the Morning Dew" — it amazed me we'd never done it before.'

Tony is currently learning a repertoire of sea shanties. While he wouldn't presume to be an identikit Stan Hugill replacement, or see himself as a genuine traditional singer ('I'm an interpreter, more in the mould of Pete Seeger') his first love *is* the sea — and enjoyment for him would be to entertain sail training associations with sea songs and shanties, encouraging youngsters in a love of shanties and their maritime heritage.

Beryl, who has borne quite a load of Spinners' administration over the years, looks to the future with both sadness and anticipation. 'Obviously, it will be a sad day for all of us when the boys finally decide to call it a day, but I can't see that happening for a while yet. And certainly we'll keep on singing.' Beryl has a brother in Australia and she and Tony would like to go out for a month when they can and visit. 'Perhaps when we're a little old man and a little old woman we'll be going to Australia every winter and playing all the old folks clubs — you never know,' she jokes.

And she adds, 'I don't live in the past. I'm looking forward to buying my motorbike and learning to ride — when I'm seventy.'

'We've been incredibly lucky over the years,' adds Cliff,' so we must have been doing something right. We wanted to introduce people to folk music, but to do it in a light and entertaining way.

'There's enough doom and gloom in the headlines these days so people don't want doom and gloom from us as well. So we try to cheer them up. And of course *nobody* comes to a Spinners' concert without getting involved. I tell them, "Even if you can't sing, you can shout — or just recite the words to the choruses."

'I'm constantly amazed anyway at the wide variety of what we call folk songs and all I want is for the people to enjoy themselves singing along with us.'

Proof that the Spinners reach people in this way is evident in the number and variety of letters they receive after every concert tour or after a TV series, from the housebound, the sick and the lonely who find their brand of entertainment a real tonic.

And with that sort of response the Spinners can't help getting involved themselves. Cliff is on the board of governors of Queen's Park School for mentally handicapped children in Lincoln, and donates a lot of time and energy to the job too, even sending each of the pupils a birthday card. And the Spinners raised £3,000 towards the cost of their swimming pool.

When Cliff sings the words from 'The Family of Man' — 'I've a brother in Melbourne, a sister in Paree' — it's almost true. In fact he's got a brother in America, and a sister in Africa, as well as his relatives in the Caribbean. So travel should figure largely in his retirement plans.

Cliff is also the oldest member of the group — he is now in his mid-fifties — and when the question is raised as to how long the Spinners can keep together, it's usually Cliff people turn to. 'Personally, I feel I'll go on as long as I feel able to. As long as the others are happy to have me, I'll carry on until we all decide to call it a day. We've still got a lot of get up and go and new audiences are discovering us every year. I think we enjoy it more now than we ever did, for we've had so much enjoyment over the years and learnt so much from our audiences that we are now able to give it back — with interest.

'To enjoy what you do is half the battle. As soon as it starts feeling like hard work, that's the time to say "Forget it" and fade away. But I don't look on what I do as a job, something I must do — I do it because I enjoy it, because I'm having fun watching other people having fun watching us.'

Mick has already taken positive steps for the future by forming his own management company — Mick Groves Management, or MGM for short! — and he's currently backing several local talents, like singer-songwriter Jack Owen, who wrote the popular 'Mist Over the Mersey'. But Mick probably won't give up performing either — 'It gets to you. It really is like a drug . . . and truthfully I enjoy it.'

In common with the rest of them, Hughie had no idea it would last this long. 'People asked me ages ago: "What will you do after all this?" I had plenty of ideas over the years, but they've all been superseded now as the success has gone on and on. You have to be a bit of an opportunist in this life, and decide at each moment what is the best idea for that time. I've no idea what's going to happen tomorrow, and I'm not too worried about it. Although I've got no money . . . but then I enjoy living beyond my means. It's good fun.

If the Spinners broke up, Hughie would probably go on performing. 'It's what I do best,' he adds. 'But it depends — if it was every single night, a different stage, a different club, I don't think I could stick it. I would probably end up neurotic or alcoholic.

'As a group we prop each other up a lot. If one of us is worried about something, or another of us has a sore throat, the others can carry the show. It must be a terribly lonely existence being a solo singer. As you get older the pressures get greater. You're constantly looking over your shoulder keeping an eye on the young contenders who are after your crown.

'But I'm not worried about the future that much.'

Clowning it up with Deryck Guyler and Harry Secombe for a 1982 Secombe with Music special from Yorkshire Television

Hughie's hornpipe, celebrating their involvement in the 1978 Tall Ships' Race

Silver Threads

'It's nice to see, in folk terms at least, that the good guys can still win . . .' Geoffrey Newson echoed the thoughts of thousands when he wrote those words in the *Daily Express* in praise of the Spinners' Silver Anniversary Year. And in terms of achievement and celebration, it was a very good year.

The Spinners began their silver jaunt abroad, when in September 1983 they headed for the west coast of America on their first transatlantic working trip. It was 'Maritime Merseyside visiting Maritime USA' as the boys gave concerts to enthusiastic crowds in such seaport venues as Baltimore's Constellation Dock, South Street Seaport, New York, and Waterside in Norfolk, Virginia.

Each was supposed to be a huge outdoor, and at times impromptu, affair. At Constellation Dock they sang before a record crowd (aided by a useful ABC network plug on both breakfast and evening news magazines) and in front of the *USS Constellation*, an eighteenth-century frigate, the oldest warship in water. At one time it fought against the English and the French simultaneously, in protest at both sides' distressing habit of each pressganging young Americans into their ranks, to carry on their colonial squabbles.

In New York they sang at Seaport where the *Wavertree* is moored. 'We especially wanted to see the *Wavertree*,' Hughie explained. 'She was built in Southampton, but sailed regularly out of the Mersey when she was owned by Leyland Brothers in Liverpool. There were great hopes at one time that the *Wavertree* might come back to Liverpool and be the centrepiece of our own Maritime Museum, but there's little hope of that now.'

She is, in fact, undergoing a million-dollar restoration, thanks to commercial sponsorship. 'It seemed to amuse more than one of the craftsmen working on her that I was actually born in Wavertree,' Hughie added. 'They couldn't get over that...'

The *Wavertree* has been joined at Seaport by the Hamburg-built *Peking*, better known this side of the Atlantic as the *Arethusa*, the name she bore when she was moored at Chatham as a floating school-ship. 'We were sad in many ways that the *Wavertree* didn't come to Liverpool,' Tony said, 'but the important thing is she is now being restored, and we look forward to the day when we can at least see her and the *Peking* racing again across the Atlantic.'

After a pleasant four days' travelling they ended their American jaunt in Virginia, where they played in the centre of Norfolk's shopping mall... and renewed friendships with the crew of the German tall ship, the *Gorch Foch*. The Spinners had competed against them in the 1978 Tall Ships Race, and in 1984, the *Gorch Foch* again crossed the Atlantic competing in yet another Tall Ships Race — on this occasion their destination was the Mersey.

In Norfolk therefore the *Gorch Foch* crew happily got into the swing of things as the Spinners launched into a spirited programme of sea-songs and shanties. 'You could say things took off when the Germans arrived,' Mick chuckled, 'and at one stage the security guards were all for stepping in and breaking up the party. But we said "No, this is the way we like it. It's just like Liverpool!"'

So as the boys played 'Can You Dance the Polka', the *Gorch Foch* crew grabbed surprised Virginia maidens and swept them off their feet, in a top-gear display which owed as much to break-dancing as it did to 'Come Dancing'.

While in the States they also renewed contact with Pete Seeger, and went to see him in concert in Washington, then it was back to England to begin their Anniversary Tour — twenty-five British venues in thirty days. It began, of course, at the Liverpool Philharmonic Hall, a night of nostalgia and nerves, recorded by Radio Merseyside for posterity and for the wider audience of their fans who could not get tickets for this sell-out celebration.

Just before the interval, 'Count' John stepped forward to pay his tribute to the lads who had become his friends over some very happy years, and signal the arrival of the anniversary cake, wheeled down the main aisle by the Spinners' wives, and decorated with a bunch of those candles which are almost impossible to blow out — as the Spinners discovered...

Undoubted high-spot of their anniversary tour was the Royal Albert Hall date in October at which they were each presented with the Gold Award of the English Folk Dance and Song Society by its director 'Nibs' Matthews. 'In doing so,' he told those who had thronged to the Hall for this unique occasion, 'the Society recognizes them as fine instrumentalists, and fine singers of folk songs and ballads, both individually and as a group. It also recognizes the active support they have given the Society over the years, and the pleasure they have given to millions.'

It was a proud and poignant moment — of the four, Hughie confessed to feeling 'numb — it didn't sink in for quite a while'; Cliff was visibly jubilant, and during the singing of 'Wild Rover', when they reached the line 'Now I'm returning with gold in great store...' he kissed his badge and shone it up again with his sleeve. Mick had a grin that would have done justice to a Cheshire cat — 'We were very, very proud. It's the one award we've received which has meant the most to us.' And Tony? 'It was the one accolade I was most proud to receive. I am more proud of it than I would be of an MBE.'

They paid tribute to those who had inspired and supported them over the years, like Sydney Carter, Alex Campbell (sadly too ill to attend), Deryck Guyler (another absentee), Red Sullivan, Bill Brown, 'Count' John, Donald Swann, many more... and they gave them everything from shanties to skiffle, from knock-about fun with 'Come Landlord Fill the Flowing Bowl' to the 'Peace Round' — even the Albert Hall anniversary set wasn't allowed to get away without joining in. Mick introduced his version of

John Lennon's 'Imagine', while Hughie took 'Scarborough Fair' and made it his own.

Backstage there was champagne and an anniversary cake and good-humoured chaos as a host of old friends dropped by. And then, next day, after a few hours' sleep, most of the group were up and out on the Thames Embankment, welcoming to London those who had been on the Peace March. It was the largest demo CND had mustered for some time — some 400,000 people converged on the capital. 'God smiled on us that day,' remembers Tony. 'If it had rained the numbers would have been decimated. As it was, it was tremendous. Chaotic, but tremendous.' And the Spinners did their bit to keep it good-humoured, playing from a make-shift stage on the back of a lorry.

This concern for the human race, and peace and harmony and the survival of black and white has been a continuing theme in the Spinners' witness, both personal and musical. It surfaced many times during their anniversary year . . . they recorded their double anniversary album *In Our Liverpool Home* live at the Phil before a free audience of the city's unemployed, and returned the following May for a concert with the Royal Liverpool Philharmonic Orchestra to raise funds for a music workshop for jobless youngsters. Then at Christmas 1984 they donated all the proceeds from their big West Country concert at Bristol's Colston Hall to the Ethiopian Famine Appeal.

Everywhere they played on their anniversary tour, they played to sell-out houses — but it hadn't always been like that. In Newcastle, where their Geordie fans have adopted Cliff as an honorary 'Newcastle Brownie', Mick recalled the early days when they struggled to hold the attention of no more than a dozen in the Wallsend Miners' Welfare Club. This was probably because it was Bingo night and they were only filling in between sessions — and also because of a persistent drunken Irish heckler, who kept asking for Irish songs they didn't know!

Bristol came up trumps when the windscreen of their van was smashed by late-night revellers. Tony and Cliff went down to investigate, and in a spontaneous Good Samaritan mood, Tony also crossed the quayside opposite the hotel, to where the same gang of revellers had vandalized a dinghy sail and left it dangling in the water. Tony leant over to lift the sodden canvas out of the dock — and his glasses fell into the water.

Half-way through a hectic tour, and with no spare pair of glasses, he was then rather desperate to get them back. The police put him on to a private diver who said he'd turn out right away, even though it was 5 a.m. So, very early next day, Mick came down to breakfast, oblivious of the night's drama, to find Tony waiting in the lobby.

'I said to him "What are you doing up so early"' Mick recalled, 'and Tony said, "I'm waiting for my diver." I thought, "Typical. That's Tony all over. You ask him a simple question . . ."'

The following spring they went back on the road to mop up those venues and reach those fans they hadn't seen before Christmas — and more drama followed them at Worthing, where the hotel they were staying in caught fire.

'Tony and I were driving back to the hotel,' remembered Cliff, 'when we both saw smoke coming from the bedroom windows. So Tony rushed into reception to raise the alarm, while I went upstairs to help shepherd some of the elderly guests to safety. I also rescued my camera and started taking pictures.'

The hotel served hot tea to those gathered on the lawns while firemen fought the blaze — and Tony serenaded them . . . and the local paper used one of Cliff's dramatic pictures on its front page the next day.

Their anniversary didn't just take in big concert halls. They found time to return, naturally, to their own folk club home at the Triton in Liverpool, where there was more champagne and another anniversary cake, and club chairman Jim Thompson presented each of them with generous tokens to be spent at a top jewellers in the city.

And the following April they went to Bradford for the anniversary of the Topic Club, one of Britain's oldest folk clubs. That too was a nice relaxed occasion — 'A good old-fashioned folk evening,' said Hughie.

In retrospect it seemed extremely fitting that Liverpool

should plan its mammoth International Garden Festival to coincide with the Spinners' Anniversary Year — certainly they were much in demand during its six-month run, attending both the Royal opening and the closing ceremony and taking part in the closing concert with the Reds and Blues Marching Band, leading the audience, Pied-Piper fashion, from the Festival site.

In between times they gave several concerts in the Arena Theatre, and recorded several shows at the Festival, with appearances on such diverse delights as 'Breakfast Time' and 'Gardeners' World'. At the Shanty Festival in August, which coincided with the visit of the Tall Ships, they joined Stan Hugill, Pete McGovern and many more in the massed 'Leaving of Liverpool' singaround as the Tall Ships sailed out. It was the most spectacular event of the summer, which brought millions cramming both banks of the Mersey — and also the most spectacular traffic jams ever seen in Liverpool or on the Wirral. Many abandoned their cars, or slept in them, and dawn was breaking the next day before the last cars could move out.

'It hasn't been easy being an Everton supporter in Liverpool these past few years,' Hughie admitted with a grin. So he was more than pleased, as were the rest of them, to be in at the turning of the tide — at Wembley in August 1984 for the great Merseyside Charity Shield extravaganza, in which Everton beat Liverpool by one flukey goal. The Spinners were not only there that day — they also sang on Wembley's sacred turf . . . 'We Shall Not Be Moved', 'In Our Merseyside Home', and the soccer anthem, 'You'll Never Walk Alone'.

In the middle of all this, they still found time to celebrate their anniversary with a wider audience on radio and television. For Christmas 1983 they recorded a programme of seasonal songs and carols for television at York's Castle Museum, and by popular demand, issued one of the songs, 'The Wind Is Blowing' (written by Liverpudlian and ex-Scaffold member John Gorman), as a single for Christmas 1984.

On radio they were guests of John Dunn and Gloria Hunniford, and also of Jim Lloyd on 'Folk Club'. Jim asked each of them how they saw the future of folk in Britain. 'It should go from strength to strength and establish itself as a real alternative,' Mick said, while Hughie added: 'If the EFDSS maintains its outward posture and singers maintain their links with the EFDSS, it can't go wrong.'

'People said folk music needed nurturing, otherwise it would die,' said Tony. 'They said it was a delicate plant... that's rubbish. It's a strong plant, but an awful lot of its leaves are delicate, and they might get burned off if we're not careful.' And Cliff urged young people to latch on to this 'precious gift of folk music, to preserve it and give it out to future generations.'

Bob Azurdia, one of Radio Merseyside's top names, commenting on their anniversary, called the Spinners 'a showbiz phenomenon'. They might not be everyone's scene but he was delighted they still had the ability 'to win over audiences more in tune with Culture Club than with culture'.

For their Silver Jubilee Party Show on Radio 2, producer John Fawcett Wilson had lined up several surprises. Deryck Guyler turned up to play his washboard in waltztime for 'In My Liverpool Home', and also read one of Pete McGovern's poems in Scouse dialect. Called 'Paddy Kelly', it is full of lost Liverpool memories, of the old Majestic and the buskers who used to play outside... 'a one-legged guitar player, a clog dancer from Wigan, a feller who whistled standin' on his hands. But my favourite was the man who played the zither — I'm sure he must have played wi' lazzie bands.'

Sydney Carter provided a real surprise by bursting into song in praise of the Spinners, full of envy for their energy and youthful charm —

'My waist is getting thicker now,
My hair is getting thinner.
But this doesn't seem to happen to you
If you are a Spinner.'

It was left to Kenny Ball and his Jazzmen to wheel on the

cake before launching into the finale with 'Maggie May'. 'For the next twenty-five years may they give us as much pleasure as they've given us over the last twenty-five,' he said.

Even though Sydney Carter's tribute ended with the words: 'Good luck I say to Liverpool and thank you for the Spinners' and even though much of their twenty-fifth anniversary year was spent singing at or promoting the hugely enjoyable and successful International Garden Festival, their home city seemed loth to reward them either for their enthusiasm or their loyalty.

Liverpool City Council seemed more keen to give the Freedom of the City to the Beatles (who in turn seemed less than keen with the idea) than to stars of the calibre of the Spinners, who have stayed closed to their Merseyside roots. Several letters of regret began appearing in the local papers, of which this one in the *Liverpool Echo* was typical. 'I don't get the impression that the Beatles are exactly leaping up and down with joy at the prospect of being honoured by their home town', wrote one fan. 'If you're talking about loyalty to Liverpool, where they still live and perform regularly, and for which they've been marvellous ambassadors both at home and abroad, then you're talking about the Spinners. To give them the Freedom of the City would be a perfect end to their anniversary year and please their legion of loyal, grateful fans.' Sadly, his plea and those of many others fell on deaf ears.

Not that it worried the Spinners unduly. They got on with the entertaining and kept the party atmosphere going in 1984 by recording a new album, *Last Night We Had A Do*, and a new series of their radio show, 'Spinners and Friends'.

The album was recorded in the studios of PRT before a live audience, recreating the sounds of a club night. 'It was suggested,' explains Mick, 'that we had a few chinking bottles in the background, so two studio hands decided the best way to do this was to chuck a crate of bottles between them! This worked all right — until they dropped it right in the middle of my verse on "Whiskey in the Jar". You can still hear the smash on the record!'

Deryck Guyler returned by popular demand to guest with them on that album, and for their radio series they invited Rolf Harris, the lovely Dana, Cy Grant, comedians Tom O'Connor and Duggie Brown, concertina virtuoso Alistair Anderson — and a special showcase featuring the talents of their very own 'Count' John McCormick.

At the end of all these celebrations, tragedy struck the Spinners' family in January 1985. Traditionally a rest month for the group, January is an ideal time for Cliff to escape to sunnier climes and visit his friends and relatives in Jamaica. His wife Janet did not go with him — she had suffered a heart attack shortly before the group's Christmas tour the previous month, and stayed at home to recuperate. All the signs looked good, yet hardly had Cliff set foot in Kingston than Janet had a relapse and died.

Riots on the normally tranquil Caribbean island made it difficult to reach Cliff and break the news — that was eventually done via the Jamaican Broadcasting Service — and then impossible for him to get an immediate flight home. It was four agonizing days before he could join his heartbroken family back on Merseyside, and before Janet, Cliff's rock and companion through almost forty years of marriage, was buried following a simple service near their Widnes home.

So at the end of the day, what did the critics make of the Spinners' Silver Jubilee, their staying power, their continued appeal, twenty-five years on? The *Liverpool Daily Post*'s folk writer, Jack Coutts, grudgingly admitted that, while they might not be the greatest of musicians or singers, nor attempt adventurous interpretations of traditional material, their appeal continued undiminished because they give people what they want — 'unsophisticated, approachable entertainment'.

Writing in the *Sunday Times*, Derek Jewell was more positive. The year 1958 had indeed been a very good one, for it spawned not only the Spinners, but the Shadows, who were also celebrating their Silver Tour in 1983 — and to cap it all, even the Animals were making a much-heralded comeback. 'To hell with nostalgia,' Jewell wrote. 'Survival is usually because of talent, humanity and charisma. So, we salute your decades of achievement.' These elder statesmen of the pop business, he added, inspired loyalty because they cared about their audiences. 'You may or may not like what they do, but they deliver always, and no messing.'

In the *Daily Express*, Geoffrey Newson added: 'In a business world which still tends to back hares rather than tortoises, the Spinners have proved everyone wrong.' It was twenty-five years, he added, of radio, television and concert tours, yet they still dashed home to Liverpool as often as they could to be with their wives and perform in their own club . . . 'and never a word of bad language in their act in twenty-five years'.

'The lads have never done daft things like dabbling in drugs, living in a cloth bag, or knocking the Royal Family. It's nice to see that, in folk terms at least, the good guys can still win.'

Discography

'When you've known the Spinners as long as I have, you'll come to realize they are not only a group, but a way of life.' (Record producer Terry Brown, in the sleeve notes of *Another LP by the Spinners*)

The following LPs have been made by the Spinners, either in studio session or live performance:

Quayside Songs Old and New (HMV — CLP 1500) 1962
Fried Bread and Brandy-o; Three Jolly Boys; Woman Sweeter than Man; Johnny Todd; Blood Red Roses; Roll, Alabama, Roll; Liverpool Girls; Wearing of the Green; Old Britannia; Champion of the Seas. Haul Away Joe; Talking Football Pools; John Peel; McCafferty; Matty Rag; The Flowers of Manchester; The Barrer Boys' Lament; I Wish I was Back in Liverpool.
(Recorded and edited by Peter Kennedy at Cecil Sharp House. The only LP also to feature Jacqui McDonald.)

The Spinners (Fontana — TL 5201) 1963
Whip Jamboree; The Farmers' Three Sons; Colun Man; Sunshine; Turpin Hero; Mandy; Barbara Allen. Liverpool Barrer Boy; Dirty Old Town; Hosanna; Marco Polo; Rata; River Bend; Lure of TV.

Folk at the Phil (Fontana STL 5219) 1964
Fried Bread and Brandy-o; John Peel; Colun Man; Woman Sweeter Than Man; Irish Rover; Silver in the Stubble; The Outlandish Knight; Aram Sa-Sa. Here's to Cheshire; The Mermaid; Little Matty Groves; Lord Randall; 'Enery My Son; Maggie May; I Wish I was Back in Liverpool.

More Folk at the Phil (Fontana STL 5234) 1965
Philimiooriay; Whiskey You're the Devil; Missa Ramgoat; Little Sally Rackett; Paddy Doyle; A Long Time Ago; Greenland Whale Fishing;

Adam in the Garden. The Ellan Vannin Tragedy; Cosher Bailey; Rukumbine; Miss Lucy; Wimoweh; Strangest Dream.
(Both 'Phil' LPs recorded at the Spinners' first Liverpool Philharmonic Hall concert, April 1964. *Folk at the Phil* released to coincide with the group's turning professional in September 1964.)

The Family of Man (Fontana STL 5361) 1966
Bold Reynolds; Liza; Dockers' Way; Blue Nose; Bonnie House of Airlie; Erev Shele Shoshanim (Evening of Roses); Las Kan Fin (Lost Can't Find); A-Roving. Liverpool Packet; Stanley and Dora; Asikatali; Teacher Lick the Gal; Three Jovial Welshmen; Van Dieman's Land; Tan Tan; The Family of Man.
(With Spike Heatley on bass.)

Another LP by the Spinners (Fontana STL 5431) 1967
Drunken Sailor*; Blood Red Roses; Sally Brown; Liverpool Judies*; Linstead Market*; Sweet William's Ghost; Navvy Boots*; Pleasant and Delightful. Jug of Punch*; Rothesay-o*;Three Jolly Boys*; Gungu Walk*; Still Growing; Minstrel Boy*; Sly Mongoose; The Leaving of Liverpool*.
(Recorded live at the Liverpool Philharmonic Hall, September 1966. Later released as *Another Spinner from the Spinners* (Fontana 6857 006) and ten tracks (*) became *Live Performance*, released in 1968 (Contour 6870 502).)

The Spinners Clockwork Storybook (Fontana SFL 13191) 1969
Uncle Sigmund's Clockwork Storybook (Stop, Look, Listen); The Fox; Abiyoyo; Olenna; 'Fraid; Long Time Ago; Sweet Potatoes; The Keeper; Mandy; Seven Little Kids.
(This later became *Stop, Look, Listen*, re-issued on Contour 6870 529.)

Not Quite Folk (Fontana STL 5495) 1969
Collier Lad; Kick the Cat; Black and White; Beautiful Cedars; Paper Bag; Talking Football Pools; Island Woman. When the Old Dun Cow Caught Fire; Been on the Road; Brown Boy; Seth Davey; Hard Case; Shoal of Herring; My Last Cigarette.
(With Brian Lemon — piano, Tony Carr — drums, Spike Heatley — bass and special guest George Chisholm who played trombone on 'The Old Dun Cow'.)

The Spinners Are In Town (Fontana 6309 014) 1970
Shine Eye Girl; Skye Boat Song; The Work of the Irish; She Moved Through the Fair; Hosanna; The Fireship; Whip Jamboree. Champion of the Seas; Liverpool Barrer Boy; Manchester Rambler; Jackass; She's Like the Swallow; Lincolnshire Poacher; Coney Island Washboard Roundalay.

(With Ron Matthewson, Brian Spring, Sheila Mason, Dennis Smith, plus Bill Brown on bass and special guest Deryck Guyler who played washboard on Coney Island.)

Love Is Teasing (EMI SCX 6493) 1972 (Re-issued EMI NTS 110)
Love is Teasing; Woman Sweeter Than Man; Waters of Tyne; To Hear the Nightingale; Soldiers Cloak; John O'Hazelgreen; Jamaica Farewell. Dance the Flora; Mek Me Hold; Banks of the Ohio; Beware, Oh Take Care; Mary Ann; Seventeen Come Sunday; The Shepherd Lad.

Sing Out, Shout With Joy (EMI SCX 6526) 1972
Lord of the Dance; Child for the World; Lullay My Liking; Mrs Houlighan's Christmas Cake; The Holly and the Ivy; The Virgin Mary Had a Baby Boy; Children Go Where I Send Thee. As I Sat Under a Sycamore Tree; Sing Out, Shout with Joy; Kids' Carols; I Wonder as I Wander; Amen; Twelve Days of Christmas; Shalom Medley; We Wish You a Merry Christmas.
(Recorded live at Bristol and Sheffield.)

By Arrangement (EMI EMC 3009) 1973
Here's to the Couple; Zombie Jamboree; Any Complaints?; Chevaliers de la Table Ronde; The Collier's Rant; Everybody Loves Saturday Night. Bucket of the Mountain Dew; The D-Day Dodgers; Perry Merry Dixie; Dip and Fall Back; When I First Came to this Land; So Long, It's been Good to Know You.
(Jimmy Powers and his ceilidh musicians joined in on 'Bucket of the Mountain Dew'. This was later re-issued as *Everybody Loves Saturday Night* on Music for Pleasure (MFP 50339))

The Spinners at The London Palladium (EMI EMC 3044) 1974
Auntie Maggie's Remedy; Poverty Knock; Widdicombe Fair; A Lover and his Lass; The Cruel Mother; Old Mother Lee; Will Ye Go Lassie Go. Deep Blue Sea; Calico Printer's Clerk; Guantanamera; Fan Me Soldier Man; Amazing Grace; Parting Glass.
(First recording to feature 'Count' John McCormick on bass.)

The Spinners' English Collection (EMI OU 2120) 1976
Come Landlord Fill the Flowing Bowl; The Bailiff's Daughter of Islington; The Coventry Carol; Jones's Ale; The Blaydon Races; The Foggy Dew; To Be a Farmer's Boy; Greensleeves/Lovely Joan; Keep Your Feet Still, Geordie Hinney. John Barleycorn; The Bedford May Carol; Twanky Dillo; Villikins and his Dinah; Four Loom Weaver; Cheshire Souling Song; North Country Maid; Brigg Fair/Harvest Home; The Derby Ram.
(Record producer Peter Vince played harpsichord on 'Lovely Joan'.)

All Day Singing (EMI EMC 3167) 1977
All Day Singing; The Moonshiner; William Brown; Bleacher Lass o' Kelvinhaugh; Jane and Louisa; Tom Brown; Castles in the Air. Lamorna; The Cobblers' Song; Ring of Iron; Waltzing Matilda; Little Boy; Muleskinner Blues; So Long, It's Been Good to Know You.
(Compiled from concerts recorded at Croydon, Bournemouth and Leicester.)

Songs of the Tall Ships (EMI NTS 154) 1978
Santy Anno; Whiskey Johnny; Spanish Ladies; Clear the Track; Portsmouth; Lowlands Away; Do Let Me Go; Roll Alabama; Stormyalong; New York Gals (Can't You Dance the Polka); Little Sally Rackett. Paddy Lay Back; Donky Riding; Old Swansea Town; Blow Boys Blow; Liverpool Hornpipe; Jackie Brown; Lime Juice Ship; Blow the Man Down; The Ebenezer; Shenandoah.
(With members of the Ocean Youth Club supplying the choruses, and Neil Wayne on concertina.)

Your 20 Favourite Christmas Carols (EMI SCX 6602) 1978
Hark the Herald Angels Sing; While Shepherds Watched Their Flocks; Silent Night; Good King Wenceslas; In Dulce Jubilo; I Saw Three Ships; In the Bleak Mid-Winter; Deck the Hall; O Little Town of Bethlehem; The First Nowell. The Sussex Carol; The Wassailing Song; Once in Royal David's City; Ding Dong Merrily on High; We Three Kings; Away in a Manger; O Come All Ye Faithful; The Rocking Carol; The Holly and the Ivy; God Rest You Merry, Gentlemen.
(With David Bell — mander organ, Brian Bennett — percussion, Alan Parker and Kevin Peek — guitars, Bob Buckle — banjo.)

Around the World and Back Again (Dingles DID 712) 1981
Derby Ram; No Tearie Jeremiah; Suliram; Botany Bay; The Wild Colonial Boy; Henry Martin; Bells of Rhymney; Rancho Grande; Brian O'Lynn; Bread and Fishes. Old Pendle; La Veille de Noel; Shenandoah; Somagwaza; This Land is Your Land; The Blantyre Explosion; Ar Lan y Mor; Go Slow; Mist Over the Mersey; Haere Ra (Now is the Hour).
('Count' John McCormick makes his recording debut as a solo vocalist on 'Suliram'.)

Here's To You... From The Spinners (PRT N145) 1982
Football Crazy; Island in the Sun; Messing About on the River; Dirty Old Town; London Roving Jack; Liverpool Lou; Here's to You Sweet England; Black and White. Eros; Kumbaya; Morning has Broken; Going to the Zoo; Seth Davey; Malaika; Sweet Thames Flow Softly; Leaving of Liverpool.

In Our Liverpool Home (PRT/SPN 1) 1983
Record One — Maggie May; Island in the Sun; Rukumbine; Johnny Todd; Creeping Jane; Roving Navvy; Lure of the Mines. Home Boys Home; Scarborough Fair; Wor Geordie's Lost His Penka; Dingle Regatta; Barnyards of Delgaty; Family of Man.
Record Two — Wild Rover; South Australia; Tom's Gone to Hilo; Haul on the Bowline; Stockholm Tar; Peace Round; Heavy Rain; Matty Rag. Imagine; Skiffle Set (Worried Man/Midnight Special/Pick a Bale of Cotton); Liverpool Home; Matchstalk Men; Black and White.
(Double album specially recorded live at the Liverpool Philharmonic Hall to celebrate their 25th anniversary).

From these recordings, a number of compilation albums have appeared over the years. They include:

The Spinners (Contour CN2026)
The Singing City (Philips 7176 074)
The Spinners Vol 1 (Contour CN2006)
The Spinners Vol 2; Black and White (Philips 6382 047)
The Spinners Vol 3; Adam in the Garden (Philips 6382 0482)
Spotlight On The Spinners (Philips 6625 014)
16 Star Tracks By The Spinners (Philips 6308 064)
From Liverpool To Coney Island (Philips SON 008)
Ten Of The Best (Fontana SFXL 51)
An Evening With The Spinners (Contour 6870 588)
The Spinners Collection (Pickwick PDA 026)
Meet The Spinners (Warwick WW 5058)
18 Golden Favourites (EMI NTS 165)
This Is The Spinners (EMI THIS 7)
Caribbean Sunshine Hits (EMI OU 2235)
20 Golden Folk Songs (EMI NTS 193)

(Most of the Spinners' albums and compilations are available on cassette, and issued on cassette only is *The Spinners* (EMI Ideal TC IDL 7) which has 21 tracks including: Blaydon Races, All Day Singing, Lord of the Dance, Last Thing on My Mind, Dip and Fall Back, Auntie Maggie's Remedy, Bucket of the Mountain Dew, Twanky Dillo and Castles in the Air.)

EPs
Songs Spun in Liverpool by The Liverpool Spinners (including Jacqui McDonald — Topic TOP 69) 1962
Whip Jamboree; The Liverpool Barrow Boy; Hayarden; Champion of the Seas; Judy Drownded; John Peel.
(Recorded at the Spinners' club in Samson and Barlow's, Liverpool.)

Apart from this The Spinners recorded three EPs for Fontana — *The Singing City* (Dirty Old Town; Orange and Green; The Leaving of Liverpool; In My Liverpool Home), *The City Sings Back* (Marco Polo; Maggie May; Liverpool Lullaby; The Harrier Song), and *Flowers of Manchester* (Flowers of Manchester; Droylsden Wakes; Sunshine; Manchester Rambler).

Singles
The Spinners have made a number of singles over the years, and these include Dirty Old Town/Philimooriay; Maggie May/Linstead Market; Family of Man/Shortness of Sight; Orange and Green/Mrs Houlighan's Christmas Cake; I've Been on the Road/Bluenose; Black and

White/Strangest Dream; Shine Eye Gal/Amen; The Old Dun Cow/Hold Him Joe; Funeral in Berlin/Diamonds and Pearls; Seth Davey/All For Me Grog; Uncle Sigmund's Clockwork Storybook/Mechanical Blackbird; Malaika/Wing Like a Dove (all for Fontana).
During their time with EMI they issued Here's to the Couple/Deep Blue Sea; Castles in the Air/Lamorna; Last Thing on My Mind/We Shall Not be Moved.

Last Night We Had a Do (PRT N6553) 1984
Whiskey in the Jar; Grannie's Old Armchair; Yellow Bird; Little Boxes; Rock Island Line; Bring a Little Water, Sylvie; Cushie Butterfield; Sloop John B. A Pub with No Beer; Midnight Special; Judy Drownded; Freight Train; The Car Song; Frankie and Johnny; Tom Dooley; The Strangest Dream; Goodnight Irene.
(Another live album in a club atmosphere with guests Colin Green — guitar, Kenny Clare — drums, and Deryck Guyler — washboard).

For PRT, they issued the Christmas single (1984) — The Wind is Blowing/The Wren Boys' Song (PRT 7P316).

Grateful thanks to John Russell of Record Enterprises, Lancing, West Sussex, for his help in compiling this discography.